William Harnett Blanch

The Blue-Coat Boys

Or, School Life in Christ's Hospital

William Harnett Blanch

The Blue-Coat Boys
Or, School Life in Christ's Hospital

ISBN/EAN: 9783337016302

Printed in Europe, USA, Canada, Australia, Japan

Cover: Foto ©ninafisch / pixelio.de

More available books at **www.hansebooks.com**

THE BLUE-COAT BOYS;

OR,

School Life in Christ's Hospital.

ETON.   CHRIST'S HOSPITAL.

PUBLIC SCHOOL BIRCHES.
ETON AND CHRIST'S HOSPITAL
PHOTOGRAPHED FROM ORIGINALS

Weight of Eton birch 12 oz.   Length of Eton birch 54 ins.
Weight of Christ's Hospital birch 3 oz. Length of Christ's Hospital birch 32 ins.

PHOTOGRAPHED BY W. GRIGGS, HANOVER ST. PECKHAM. REGISTERED.

THE BLUE-COAT BOYS;

OR,

School Life in Christ's Hospital.

WITH

A SHORT HISTORY OF THE FOUNDATION.

BY

WILLIAM HARNETT BLANCH,

AUTHOR OF "THE HISTORY AND ANTIQUITIES OF CAMBERWELL,"
"THE HISTORY OF DULWICH COLLEGE," &c.

LONDON:
E. W. ALLEN, AVE MARIA LANE, E.C.
1877.

LONDON:
BRADBURY, AGNEW, & CO., PRINTERS, WHITEFRIARS.

TO

J. D. ALLCROFT, Esq.,

TREASURER OF CHRIST'S HOSPITAL,

𝕿his 𝕭ook is 𝕴nscribed

IN GRATEFUL RECOLLECTION OF EIGHT HAPPY YEARS

SPENT IN CHRIST'S HOSPITAL,

AND AS

A SLIGHT BUT HEARTY ACKNOWLEDGMENT OF THE GREAT BENEFITS

DERIVED FROM INSTRUCTION THEREIN RECEIVED.

PREFACE.

THE materials for this little book were put together eighteen months ago, when, at the request of the much-respected President of the London Short-hand Writers' Association, T. J. Woods, Esq., I delivered a Lecture on "Christ's Hospital," at St. John's Gate, before my good friends, the members of that useful Association.

Substantially, it has now been printed as written and delivered, with an introductory chapter added thereto. I have—to give a more extended view of School Life—quoted from the writings of Coleridge, Lamb, Leigh Hunt, and others, in order that the contrast between Christ's Hospital as it was, and as it is, may be more effectually set forth.

W. H. B.

CONTENTS.

CHAP.		PAGE
I.—THE FOUNDER		1
II.—EARLY HISTORY		8
III.—SCHOOL BUILDINGS		15
IV.—PECULIAR BEQUESTS		22
V.—FAMOUS BLUES		29
VI.—SCHOOL LIFE AT HERTFORD		40
VII.—SCHOOL LIFE IN LONDON		56
VIII.—SCHOOL PUNISHMENT.—FLOGGING		63
IX.—SCHOOL FOOD		72
X.—GRECIANS AND MONITORS		81
XI.—BEADLES AND NURSES		89
XII.—SCHOOL SLANG AND LITERATURE		95
XIII.—CHAFFING		100
XIV.—HOLIDAYS AND FRIENDLESS BOYS		102
XV.—SUNDAY AT SCHOOL AND THE INFIRMARY		105
XVI.—EASTER CEREMONIES AND PUBLIC SUPPERS		108
XVII.—BULLIES, FAGS, AND FAGGING		112
XVIII.—THE TRADES.—"HOUSEY MONEY."—THE TUCK SHOP		121
XIX.—AMICABLE, BENEVOLENT, AND OTHER BLUES		125

ILLUSTRATION.

PUBLIC SCHOOL BIRCHES . . . . . *Frontispiece*

INTRODUCTORY.

THE sad end of poor little William Arthur Gibbs has brought Christ's Hospital, its past history and present state of discipline and government, prominently before the public. I do not propose to enter into the merits of the particular case which has created such a painful impression on the public mind, inasmuch as I should write without a full knowledge of the facts; and in the next place a committee of distinguished men, in whose impartiality and judgment all must have confidence, has been appointed with ample powers to make the fullest and most searching inquiry.

I desire, however, in the following pages, to place on record some account of the School, as it was in the days of Lamb and Coleridge, and Leigh Hunt, to give my recollections from 1843—51, and to state briefly the improvements which have taken place since that time; for I have never ceased to take the liveliest interest in the Foundation, and to note all that has been done within its cloistered, calm retreat.

Of late, having a son on the Foundation, I have had personal reasons for making a more minute investigation.

At the outset, then, I may state boldly, and without the slightest hesitation, that, in my opinion, many of the statements which have been published in the newspapers, are grossly exaggerated pictures of Christ's Hospital life; and further, it does appear to me to be most unfair to draw pictures of school life twenty, thirty, or forty years ago, and pass them off as a reflex of the school life of to-day. In giving my experience of both past and present, I do not wish specifically to contradict what others have written, but I do desire to let the public know that there are "old Blues" who regard their school with affection, and who look back upon their school days without a shudder. Out of the many thousands of boys educated at Christ's Hospital, there must of necessity have been many who, from some special cause, some infirmity of temper, or idiosyncracy, or, it may be, from social surroundings, or non-appreciation by masters, or bad treatment by school-fellows and other causes, were not happy, and whose reminiscences of school life are not agreeable. But I think I may state without fear of contradiction, that the great majority of "Blues" look back upon their school days with unalloyed pleasure. For myself, I may state that the eight years spent in Christ's Hospital were the happiest eight years of my life, notwithstanding the fact that from choice I occupied the position which is now being held up as something very shocking and repulsive in school life—that of fag. I filled almost every position in the school, from monitor's fag to that of monitor; and, as I have explained in another page, the position of fag in my time was much sought after, as it gave us certain privileges and perquisites.

Fagging, as it is carried on at Christ's Hospital, must not be confounded with Winchester "Tunding," nor must it be associated with thrashing, and bullying, and ill-treatment, as it is in other public schools.

And then as regards flogging, an entire misconception appears to exist as to the extent to which birching is now carried out in Christ's Hospital. In my time, say twenty-five years ago, the birch was certainly to some extent used by the assistant masters; one of whom was, I believe, dismissed for using it without discretion.

All is now changed. Flogging is now only resorted to in cases of grave moral delinquencies; and I find from inquiry that for some years past the average annual number of floggings has been only eight in a school of eight hundred, and the well-known character of the present Head Master, the Rev. R. Lee, is sufficient guarantee that the government of the school will be eminently tolerant and just.

I must confess it would be better if these floggings were "none at all;" but those who know anything of public schools must admit that grave offences against morality must at all times be severely punished, and that publicly, and with due official solemnity; or vicious habits would become general, and lasting injury would be done to the tone of the school and to individual character.

Whilst crime exists, punishment must of necessity be carried out; and if this is necessary in the great world outside, how much more necessary is it in school life, where character is being moulded and habits formed? I would not assert that flogging is the best mode of punishment that could be devised. I do not think it is—indeed, it is to my mind a barbarous anachronism—and he would be a benefactor who would devise a new method of punishment.

It must, however, be borne in mind that the birch is used in all schools, and is not peculiar to Christ's Hospital; that it is now but seldom used either in the London or Hertford school; and that the dreadful instrument of torture, about which so much has been written, is only $3\frac{1}{2}$ ounces in weight, and 32 inches long, whilst the rods used in other public schools are nearly four times the weight, and about twice the length.

I procured a rod from the London authorities a few days since, and it agrees both in weight and length with one I obtained from one of the beadles about two years ago, when making inquiry into the subject for materials for a lecture.

So far then, I think, it may be admitted that the number of birchings that have taken place in Christ's Hospital are less numerous than in other schools, and that the instrument used is not beyond a boy's years to bear. With respect to the "brushing," so graphically described by the Rev. A. A. W. Drew, my respected neighbour, I must, with all due deference to him, think that his kindly and sympathetic nature has induced him somewhat to overdraw the picture. Mr. Drew and I were contemporaries at the school; we were often associated together in sports and athletic exercises; and when I was captain of my ward, Mr. Drew was also captain of his little army. Our observations of school life were, therefore, made at the same time, and yet how different are our experiences! "The beadles," says Mr. Drew, "thrashed the boys with might and main;" and one is described as having "split his shirt-sleeve right down" with the violence he used, whereas I saw no torn shirt-sleeves; and although I have seen a few birchings, I never saw a beadle "lay it on with might and main." I have seen beadles feign "laying it on," and whenever my old friend Tice wielded the rod, he systematically carried out the seeming violence, whilst in reality he was sparing the boy as much as possible. Mr. Drew has such unpleasant recollections of Christ's Hospital that he would not accept a presentation if it were offered him; but unless I am very much misinformed, the boy Blount, whose flogging twenty-five years ago has been made the sensation of to-day, has recently applied to more than one Governor for a presentation for his own son. As for myself, I have one boy in the School already, and his brother, a sturdy little fellow of eight years, is so delighted with his brother's stories of school life, that he is daily beseeching me to get him also admitted, and nothing but the opportunity is wanting to comply with his desire.

I think, then, that the parents whose faith in the Institution has of late been shaken, may be assured that school life in Christ's Hospital is not all "fagging and bullying and birching;" that presentations are as much sought after as ever; and that the discipline within the School is of the mildest possible character.

Amongst other charges, I may mention that the dress—the most conservative feature of the School—has felt the power of change. The "Blues," to their great delight, have had the yellow petticoat improved out of existence; the little useless nondescript kind of cap, which all were compelled to carry about, no longer worries the boys; and new coats are now served out twice a-year, instead of once, as in my time. Gone too are the wooden bowls and trenchers, and the leathern jacks and piggins; and Peerless Pool, with its refreshing memories, is no longer considered a portion of Christ's Hospital, but in its place the boys have a magnificent swimming bath within the walls,—a privilege which is much prized. The bath has this peculiarity about it—it is situate in three parishes.

Great changes for the better have taken place also in the School diet. The two non-meat days, Tuesday and Saturday, have disappeared from the calendar, and the boys have now not only an ample but a varied supply of food.

I state this advisedly, after having instituted the strictest inquiries on the subject. Oliver may now ask for more in Christ's Hospital without shocking any one's feelings, and what is more, he gets what he asks for. In my time we had our "mutton days," "pudding days," "soup days," and so on; and knowing what was in store for us we would enter the dining-hall with a kind of unpleasant foretaste of our allotted meal, especially if it happened to be a lean day. Now, a boy has no knowledge of the kind of dinner which is in store for him, and the speculation, I can well imagine, is provocative of hunger and desire. And then the changes of food, how delightful! Another innovation!—two kinds of vegetables are now served out, to say nothing of Yorkshire pudding and other added luxuries. Indeed, the present race of Blues are fed in right royal style, and no one, I should think, either in or out of the School, can be found bold enough to find fault with it.

Numerous modifications and improvements have been made of late years, among which may be mentioned:

Head Master substituted for Upper Grammar Master, and Orders for Grammar School thoroughly revised, December, 1866.

Head Master's authority to include superintendence not only of the whole of the Schools and Studies of the Hospital, but of the Discipline both in and out of School, 1868.

Warden's Charge revised, 1868.

Preparation School introduced, 1869.

Half-yearly reports to parents introduced, 1868—69.

Extension of admission and leaving ages, and introduction of graduated Entrance Examinations, 1869.

Again limited and regulated, 1874.

Dropping of Greek to all below Upper Grammar School, 1869.

French extended to all the London School, 1869.

Chemical Instruction and Natural Science teaching, 1869.

Introduction of German, 1871.

Authority of the chief Grammar Master (now called Head Master) at the Hertford Establishment made to extend over the studies of both School divisions there, 1869.

Enlargement of Head Master's study to enable him to have lectures there, or address a considerable number of boys at one time, 1873.

Singing and Musical Instruction much extended, 1869.

Revision of Regulations and Qualifications of boys admitted on Royal Mathematical Foundation, 1873—4.

Girls' School reorganised in 1875.

As regards the future, I have little doubt in my own mind that the authorities will sooner or later follow the example of Charterhouse, and seek a home for Christ's Hospital in the country. When such a proposition is again made, it will no doubt be carried to a successful issue, since it was lost by only fourteen votes when it was discussed in 1870; and recent events will greatly assist the advocates of removal.

The letter to the *Times*, just penned by the late esteemed Head-Master of Christ's Hospital, the Rev. G. C. Bell, cannot fail to have great influence with the Governors when considering this question. Mr. Bell points out that:

"In most boarding schools the Assistant-Masters take a large share in the control of the boys out of school hours. But at Christ's Hospital their duties usually end when the lessons are over, and the majority of them live at a distance. In the school itself the only resident members of the teaching staff are the Head Master and the chief French Master. Some six or seven others live in houses adjacent to the Hospital, and some years ago a few of them voluntarily consented to undertake the duty of visiting the wards or dormitories. It has, however, been difficult to arrange definitely their relation to the Warden, who is the person directly charged with the discipline of the school. In this work he is aided by an assistant, and is subject to the general superintendence of the Head Master. The boys are divided into wards of some forty to forty-five boys, each under the care of a matron and three monitors, boys of fifteen or sixteen years of age. A 'Grecian' has a study in each ward, and the matron may appeal to him for help, if necessary. Of the matrons I have every reason to speak with respect and sympathy. In the discharge of their duties they display admirable patience and courage, but they naturally are not so well qualified as masters to exert moral and intellectual influence over the boys; and it is impossible for the Warden, with all his energy, to make his influence constantly felt in every one of the sixteen wards."

The removal of the School will of course be a serious break in the sentiment and tradition of the place; and Old Blues, whilst giving their adhesion to the scheme on the grounds of policy and prudence, will nevertheless regretfully acknowledge its necessity.

At the same time, it must be confessed that London is rather a battle-field for men than a training-ground for boys. "Any public-school man," says Mr. Fearon, "who looks in at the quadrangle of Christ's Hospital, when the boys are out of school, must have been struck by the fact that the Blue-coat boys do not know how to play. The surface of the quadrangle and court is too hard for any violent game, and consequently one sees with astonishment big boys of thirteen and fourteen years old playing with peg-tops, whip-tops, and marbles; while those whose higher position in the school does not allow them to indulge in such amusements are reduced to lounging about the courts." Although there is much force in all this, it must yet be stated that matters have much improved since Mr. Fearon's report appeared eight years ago. The boys have now a splendid field at Dulwich for football and cricket. A gymnasium has been liberally fitted up on the site of the old Compter Prison, and visitors to the annual Athletic Sports at Dulwich are soon convinced that the young athletes can now do something more than spin tops and play at marbles. Clubs for swimming, boating, &c., have been formed, and are much patronized by the boys; and everything is now done by the authorities to encourage the youngsters to engage in manly and vigorous sports. The fact still remains, however, that instead of having facilities for indulging in many of their healthy out-door amusements, the boys have to make pilgrimage to Dulwich and elsewhere—and that only on two days in the week, Wednesday and Saturday—before reaching the play-ground.

On other days, the big and little boys are cloistered together, and if there is any tendency to bullying, there is ample time and opportunity for its practice. And then again, the removal of the School would enable the Governors to carry out a much more perfect system of surveillance out of school, by providing houses for the Assistant Masters, who would then be enabled to co-operate with the Warden in performing the duties attached to the domestic or moral government of the Institution.

At present the Masters have the control of the boys during school hours only; and as soon as the boys pass out of school, they become subject to the rule of the Warden, who is assisted by the Grecians, monitors, nurses, and beadles. Of the manner in which the duties of the Steward, or Warden, as he is now called, have been performed, I desire to bear my humble but hearty testimony. It would perhaps have been impossible for the authorities to select two more able, kindly, and eminently suitable men for the position than the late Steward, Mr. George Brooks, and the present Warden, Major Brackenbury; but when this is granted, it must nevertheless be acknowledged that the system of dual government, as at present carried out, is not the most satisfactory that could be devised, as the boy's character is cut up as it were into two parts one half of which is known only to the Warden, and the other half to the Master, whereas it cannot be doubted that the whole of the boy's character and disposition should be thoroughly understood by his superior authority.. I should be wanting in common gratitude were I to omit mention of the great services rendered to the Institution by Mrs. Oliver, the Head Matron, who has for nearly thirty years done all that a woman could do to make the boys comfortable and contented.

In conclusion, the Religious, Royal, and Ancient Foundation of Christ's Hospital has been made what it is—built up so to speak—during 300 years, by loving and devoted hands. From time to time it has attracted to itself the sympathies of the benevolent, whose munificent donations were given, not to perpetuate a kind of ragged school, as one division of it undoubtedly was in the time of King Edward, nor a purely elementary school, as some would make it now; but rather to encourage, foster, and perpetuate an institution altogether unique in its character, giving not only education, but daily sustenance and support. A mere ragged school, or a rate-supported school for educational purposes only, would never have attracted to itself, as Christ's Hospital has done, the sympathies and patronage of the public.

Christ's Hospital is an institution without a parallel in the country, and entirely *sui generis*. It is a grand relic of the mediæval spirit, a monument of the profuse munificence of that spirit, and of that constant flow of individual beneficence which clusters round an institution of such a character. It has kept up its main features, its traditions, its antique ceremonics, its peculiar dress, its rigid conservatism, its *esprit de corps*, for a period of more than three centuries. It has a long and goodly list of worthies, and it is quite as strong as Eton, and Harrow, and Winchester, in the affection of those who have been brought up in the School.

I can fairly claim for Christ's Hospital, that it has left its mark upon national history; that its sons have acquitted themselves right nobly—that wherever wealth is to be accumulated, honour to be achieved, glory won, industry to be rewarded, or the national character to be upheld, the Blues have been conspicuously to the fore.

I have endeavoured in a brief manner to indicate the gradual changes which have come over the School, and the transfer by that change of the benefits of the Hospital, from the lowest to the middle class, from the "destitute and miserable" to the "professional and commercial."

At one time a kind of pauper school, into which infants of two weeks were admitted, Christ's Hospital, owing, partly to the poor law of Elizabeth, and more perhaps to the liberality of its supporters, gradually shook off its pauper element, and became a semigrammar school for the sons of freemen only, until it became what it now is, a grand national institution.

Great changes and many improvements have recently taken place in Christ's Hospital, and still further changes are contemplated.

The future school may be cut up into Metropolitan day schools, into country boarding schools, or its immense revenues may be handed over to the School Board for London, for the benefit of the metropolitan ratepayer; and, notwithstanding its traditions, Christ's Hospital may be brought down to the level of a Board School. I say "may," because all things are possible.

For myself, I have faith in the future which awaits it. I believe it will be more useful, more successful, and more glorious in the future than it has been in the past. I have no fear that the Legislature will approve any scheme which may tend to degrade the status of Christ's Hospital; but I have a large hope that before long, through the inevitable growth of its revenues, more particularly of that portion of its funds specially left for educational purposes only, and through the impetus which School Boards must inevitably give to middle-class education, if the middle classes of this country are to retain their position; and through judicious reforms from within, Christ's Hospital will become a great public school, a worthy rival of Eton, and Winchester, and Harrow.

It can then open its doors to the more deserving scholars of the numerous elementary schools throughout the country, and thus become the head of a vast educational system, worthy of its past history and traditions.

W. H. B.

THE BLUE-COAT BOYS;

OR,

School Life in Christ's Hospital.

WITH A SHORT HISTORY OF THE FOUNDATION.

CHAPTER I.

THE FOUNDER.

IT may be a bold assertion to make, but circumstances warrant the statement, that probably no educational institution in Great Britain has a more interesting history, or one more intimately connected with events of worldwide importance, than the magnificent foundation known formally and officially as Christ's Hospital, and familiarly to every Londoner as the Blue-Coat School. Like most other of our ancient English institutions, whether judicial, political, social, religious, or educational, it is a growth rather than a creation; it is a development whose successive stages can be as clearly traced as the series of changes that, from the tiny acorn, build up the majestic oak. It was never turned out of any intellectual workshop a complete, and finished, and perfectly proportioned specimen of art—like, for instance, an utterly impracticable, but strictly logical, French Constitution—but, such as we see it, it is the work of many men and of many ages. In many respects eminently conservative, the Blue-

Coat School has, nevertheless, adapted itself to the requirements of successive generations, and is only rigidly mechanical in the observance of certain customs, and formal in respect of the mediæval garb that its inmates still wear, and the disappearance of which would be regretted by all admirers of old traditions.

Having a history, in one shape or other, extending over upwards of six centuries; numbering amongst its many benefactors persons of all ranks, from kings, queens, and princes, to citizens and city dames; surviving strange vicissitudes of fortune and angry storms of fate; springing into fresh and vigorous life immediately after undergoing the severest rigours of adversity; growing and prospering generation after generation, century after century—Christ's Hospital has proved itself an institution as hardy as in some respects it is peculiarly English, and so many distinguished names are intimately connected with its very interesting story, that it is difficult, with due regard to accuracy, to describe any one individual as pre-eminently the founder.

By general consent, however, this proud title is given to the boy king, Edward VI., and not undeservedly, for it is to him mainly that the existence of Christ's Hospital in its present shape, and for its present purposes, is due. Of the previous history of the foundation—the Monastery of the Grey Friars, established in the first half of the thirteenth century—we shall speak in a subsequent chapter. Here we have to do with the founder of the modern institution, and with the circumstances which led to its establishment.

In the clean sweep made by King Henry VIII. of monastic institutions, the Monastery of the Grey Friars in London was done away with, and the church converted into a storehouse for the reception of prizes taken from the French; but the general reduction of religious houses, where alms were regularly distributed to the poor, occasioned so much distress and such wide-spread destitution, that even the hard heart of Henry was touched; and, having despoiled the original owners, he kindly gave, by letters patent to the mayor, commonalty, and citizens, and their successors, "the church and house of the late Grey Friars within the city, and all the appurtenances thereunto belonging."

The gift, however, lay dormant for a considerable time, and it was not till 1552, when Edward VI., at the time a boy of fifteen, had been about six years on the throne, that anything was done in the matter. Edward then, moved by an appeal from Bishop Ridley, and "understanding that a great number of poor people did swarm in this realm, and chiefly in the City of London, and that no good order was taken of them," sent for the Bishop, and that prelate subsequently, by command of the King, conferred with the Corporation, one result, amongst others, being the establishment of Christ's Hospital, by the confirmation of the eighth Henry's grant of the old Grey Friars' monastery, for the sustenance and education of youth. Edward also consented to the City's petition that they might take, in mortmain, or otherwise, without licence, lands to the yearly value of ——; and, with the piety which always distinguished him, on filling up the blank with the words "4,000 marks," the young king said, before the whole Council, "Lord, I yield Thee most hearty thanks that Thou hast given me life thus long, to finish this work to the glory of Thy name." A month after signing the Charter of Incorporation, the young king, the founder of the Blue-Coat School, expired in the arms of Sir Henry Sydney, praying God to receive his spirit, and to defend the realm from Papistry. "In the foundation of Christ's Hospital," says its historian, the Rev.

William Trollope, " he had provided the surest means, under Providence, for the success of his prayer; and his life was spared just long enough to greet him with the promise of that harvest which this seminary of sound learning and true religion was destined to yield. Instigated by the pious example of their Royal benefactor, the citizens proceeded vigorously with the necessary repairs of the old canonical edifice, which, in less than six months, had sufficiently advanced to allow of the admission of 340 children in the month of November. They were clothed in livery of russet cotton; and, on the Christmas Day following, they lined the procession of the Lord Mayor and aldermen to St. Paul's, from Lawrence Lane westward. In the month of June, 1553, the young king received the corporation at the Palace, and presented them with the charter; the children also being present at the ceremony. A more interesting spectacle, connected, as it was, with the recent change in the national religion, can scarcely be conceived. Nothing so heart-stirring in its nature has, probably, occurred either before or since, even in the pleasing exhibitions of the more extended train of children in their annual processions at Easter."

The ancients would have said that King Edward VI. was beloved of the Gods, since he, dying young, yet lived long enough to establish a reputation for great ability, for pious zeal, and for an amiable disposition, while he was spared the temptation of marring by the vices of manhood the promise of his youth, or of sullying a fame which, though necessarily crude and immature, is nevertheless, so far as it goes, pure and unsullied. The Tudor sovereigns were all exceptionally able, and all made right royal rulers; but of the whole five the founder of the Blue-Coat School alone possessed a disposition at once singularly generous, sweet, and sympathetic. A precocious child, such as Edward undoubtedly was, especially if he happens to be born in the purple, is in great danger of becoming obstinate and self-opinionated—a duodecimo edition of all the talents, if not of all the virtues—but the young King's nature was, apparently, at once too broad and too deep to allow him to be easily spoiled. Perhaps if he had learned a little less and played a great deal more he would have lived longer, and the promise displayed by the boy might have ripened into the ample performance of manhood. That he was spared no pains or trouble in the acquirement of learning and accomplishments on account of his princely birth is evident from a letter written by his tutor, Dr. Coxe, in 1545, when the royal pupil was only eight years of age. In this letter the learned doctor says of the Prince:—

"He hath expugned and utterly conquered a great number of the captains of Ignorance. The eight parts of speech he hath made them his subjects and servants, and can decline any manner of Latin noun, and conjugate a verb perfectly, unless it be anomalum. These parts, thus beaten down and conquered, he beginneth to build them up again, and frame them after his purpose with due order of construction. . . . .

"He understandeth and can frame well his three concords of grammar, and hath made already forty or fifty pretty Latin verses, and can answer well favouredly to the parts, and is now ready to enter into Cato, to some proper and profitable fables of Æsop, and other wholesome and godly lesson that shall be devised for him."

That the founder of Christ's Hospital was docile and affectionate we have abundant evidence from his letters still extant, one of which, without date, but apparently written about the year 1546, to the then Queen, Katharine Parr, is as follows:—

"Most honorable and entierly beloved mother, I have me most humbli recommended unto youre grace, with lyke thankes, both for that your grace ded accepte so gentylly my simple and rude letters, and also that it pleased your grace so gentylly to vowchsaufe to directe unto me your loving and tendre letters, which do geve me much comfort and encouragement to go forward in such thinges wherin your grace bereath me on hand that I am already entered.

"I pray God I maie be hable in part to satisfy the good expectation of the Kinges Majesti my father and of your grace: whom God have ever in his most blessed keping.

"Your loving sonne,
"E. PRINCE."

That the piety of King Edward was rational and well grounded—an intelligent and reasoning, as distinguished from a superstitious piety,—is proved by the following anecdote, mentioned by Strype:—

"At the Coronation of King Edward, which was on Shrove-Sunday, February 20, 1547, an author that wrote about these times [Bal. de Viris Illustrib.] relates that he heard it from credible hands, that when three swords were brought, signs of his being king of three kingdoms, he said, there was one yet wanting. And when the nobles about him asked him what that was, he answered, *The Bible*. 'That book,' added he, 'is the sword of the Spirit, and to be preferred before these swords. That ought in all right to govern us, who use them for the people's safety by God's appointment. Without that sword, we are nothing, we can do nothing, we have no power. From that we are what we are this day. From that we receive whatsoever it is that we at this present do assume. He that rules without it, is not to be called God's minister, or a King. Under that we ought to live, to fight, to govern the people, and to perform all our affairs. From that alone we obtain all power, virtue, grace, salvation, and whatsoever we have of divine strength.' And when the pious young King had said this, and some other like words, he commanded the Bible, with the greatest reverence, to be brought and carried before him."

Pious, thoughtful, and learned, the young King also had a touch of genuine and genial humour, born of the fulness, generosity, and sympathy of his nature. A story told by Fuller shows that Edward could think and judge for himself promptly, and with a full appreciation of the motives of those by whom he was surrounded. "A covetous courtier," Fuller says, "complained to King Edward VI., of Christ College in Cambridge, that it was a superstitious foundation, consisting of a master and twelve fellows, in imitation of Christ and his twelve apostles. He advised the King also to take away one or two fellowships, so to discompose that superstitious number. 'Oh, no,' said the King, 'I have a better way than that to mar their conceit, I will add a thirteenth fellowship unto them;' which he did accordingly, and so it remaineth unto this day."

It may have been well for himself that this Prince, so religious, so practical, so accomplished, and so genial, should have died when he did. Young as he was, he has left a reputation which entitles his name to be enrolled equally amongst English worthies as amongst English kings. In the son of Jane Seymour the cause of education had a devoted friend, and of Edward VI. it should be remembered, to his eternal honour, that, dying at the age of sixteen, he reared for himself an imperishable monument, as well by the foundation of Christ's Hospital in London, as by endowing no less than sixteen grammar schools—many of them still valuable institutions—in various parts of the country.

CHAPTER II.

EARLY HISTORY.

BEFORE the dissolution of religious houses, the monasteries, with their various appendages, are calculated to have occupied within the city, nearly two-thirds of the entire area; and about one-fifth of the whole population is supposed to have been cloistered within their walls, and so the destruction of the monasteries dried up innumerable sources of charity, and deluged the city with a large floating population of mendicants; and Sir Richard Gresham, Lord Mayor of London, and father of the great civic benefactor of that name, addressed a letter to the king setting forth the extent of the prevailing distress, and praying for the appropriation of some portion of the monastic property to its relief. And in 1545, Bishop Ridley, in a sermon at Paul's Cross, announced the king's gift of the Conventual Grounds and Buildings formerly occupied by the Grey Friars, "for the reliefe of the poore." The gift was specified in an indenture executed between Henry VIII. and the Mayor and Commonalty of London, bearing date December 27th, 1545, and afterwards confirmed by Letters Patent, whereby the said Grey Friars Church, with all the edifices and grounds, the fratry, the library, the dortor, the chapter-house, the great cloister and the lesser, tenements, gardens, and vacant grounds, lead, stone, iron, &c., the Hospital of St. Bartholomew in West Smithfield, the church of the same, the lead, bells, and

Early History.

ornaments of the said hospital, with all the messuages, tenements and appurtenances, were made over to the Mayor and Commonalty for ever.

The parishes of St. Nicholas in the Shambles, St. Ewin's, and so much of St. Sepulchre as lay within Newgate, were united into one parish, for the use of which the Conventual Church was left standing, and those of St. Nicholas and St. Ewin's were destroyed. In its new capacity the church was dedicated to our Blessed Lord, under the designation of "Christ Church, founded by King Henry VIII." "A very odd foundation," says Stevens, "to let two churches out of four stand, subverting the other two, and a good hospital, and to call himself a founder!"

Henry's foundation "for the relief of the poor" was not particularly successful; the City was still the scene of much poverty; and mendicity yet abounded within its walls.

The citizens, we are told, "fell upon the Reparation and filling up of the Fryars," but the buildings had been allowed to fall into decay, and King Henry's gift was practically a dead letter.

But better days were coming for the occupants of the Grey Friars, for Henry was no more, and Jane Seymour's son, Edward, reigned in his stead.

Edward, as all students of history know, was an amiable, impressionable, and religious lad; and on one occasion, when only nine years of age, so impressed was he with the responsibilities of his position, through hearing a sermon delivered in Westminster Abbey on the grand subject of "Charity," by Bishop Ridley, that at the conclusion of the service he sent for the prelate to ask counsel and advice, and begged him to speak his mind openly and without reservation. Ridley pointed to the neglected school established by his father, and the young king forthwith wrote to the Lord Mayor concerning it. Now Ridley evidently knew how to approach a City magnate, for he forthwith repaired to the Lord Mayor, and arranged a dinner for the morrow, at which to take the king's letter into consideration. The dinner party included the Lord Mayor, Bishop Ridley, two aldermen and six commoners, and the plan of the future school was settled by these worthies over their wine, and Christ's Hospital was soon after founded by Royal Charter.

In the year 1557, four years only after the establishment of the Hospital, two distinct classes were received under its protection, and the Court Record divides the 400 boys then in the Hospital as follows:— 250 children who were to "lodge and learn," and 150 "suckling children;" and mention is made, in 1572, of "foundlings and those taken in from poverty or sickness to be maintained at the citie coste." Before being put forth to any faculties, service, or occupation, "it was ordered that being mere children, they should write and reade and caste accomptes, and be found apte thereunto; but such of the children as be pregnant, and very apte to learning, be received and kept in the Grammar Schole, in hope of preferment to the Universitie."

The hospitals of Bridewell and St. Thomas were founded at the same time as Christ's Hospital, and their revenues were at first derived from a common fund; and strange to relate, the authorities of Christ's Hospital have never been able to trace the receipt by the Hospital of any portion of the king's bounty; and Dr. Haig Brown, in his evidence before the Commissioners, went so far as to say that the Hospital had not received the Charter money. The whole cost, therefore, of conducting the school was from the first cast upon the citizens. This is a pertinent fact, and one which cannot be too closely pressed upon the attention of those who allege that Christ's Hospital should still remain a kind of superior ragged school.

Early History.

This fine institution has been built up by the great middle class of England, and the school has been moulded and modelled by those who have sustained and perpetuated it; and so far as its history can be traced, it would appear that the government of the school, by its middle-class patrons, has for centuries been eminently wise and judicious. It was perhaps fortunate when Bishop Ridley pleaded the cause of the poor before the king, that Sir Richard Dobbs was the chief magistrate of the city, for he entered with much zeal into all the plans of the prelate, became a benefactor, and persuaded many wealthy citizens to follow his good example; and, shortly before the martyrdom of Ridley, that worthy prelate penned a noble eulogium on his generous friend, commencing thus : " O Dobbs, Dobbs, Alderman and Knight, thou in thy yeare did win my heart for evermore ; " and underneath a portrait of Sir Richard Dobbs, now in the possession of the Governors, the Alderman's good deeds are thus quaintly recorded :

> Christe's Hospitall erected was a passinge dede of pittie,
> What time Sir Richard Dobbs was Maior of thys most fam[d] citie ;
> Who careful was in government, & furthered much the same
> Also a benefactor good, and joyed to see it frame :.
> Whose portraiture heare his friends have sett, to put each wight in minde
> To imitate his vertuous dedes as god hath us assinde.

Sir Richard Dobbs was mainly instrumental in persuading the citizens to support the school by means of ward collections, and the money so collected was mainly appropriated to support the very poor who found refuge within the walls of the Hospital, for at this time the school bore the two-fold character of a grammar school and an asylum for those whom we should now denominate pauper children.

A trace of the original pauper character of one

part, at least, of the institution may be discerned in the proceedings of 1624, when "the Lord Mayor having proposed to send children into the hospital under twelve years of age, who were found begging in the streets, the knights and aldermen of the hospital were ordered to attend the Court of Aldermen thereon." On the other hand, the order of the same year, that no children should be admitted unless their parents should be free of the city of London, is evidence that the Governors considered themselves to possess the right to determine the qualification of the children who were to be admitted, and that the Hospital was not a place for the indiscriminate reception of the poor.

The ward collections, which were, after all, a kind of voluntary poor-rate, went for the support of the very poor; and the benefactions of the middle class were appropriated to the support of freemen's children; and as the ward collections fell off, so did the very poor element within the walls decrease, and the school became a kind of City Grammar School.

This result was, no doubt, partly to be attributed to the Poor Law of Elizabeth, superseding as it did the authority of the Governors of the Royal Hospital as Guardians of the Poor of the City of London.

In 1652, a century after the foundation, it was "ordered that no children shall be admitted, but those who are sons of freemen," and it was not until 1745 that a Governor was allowed, in every four turns, to present one child whose father was not free of the city of London.

In 1765 the rule in favour of non-free children was again enlarged to one non-free child in three turns (clergymen's children being accounted free); in 1828 it was again extended to one turn in two; and in 1839 the distinction between free and non-free was totally abolished, the Hospital being thereby open to all classes of children, without any preference in favour of persons belonging to the City of London.

In addition to the ward collections, and the donations of private benefactors, the Hospital derived funds from two Acts of Common Council passed in 1554, one repressing, under certain penalties, the gross profanations which then prevailed in St. Paul's Cathedral; the other restricting in like manner, the enormous expenses of civic entertainments, "one moiety of such pains and penalties being," in both cases, "to Christ's Hospital within Newgate, and the other half to him that will sue for the same in any court of record within the city."

By an Act of Common Council, so early as the reign of Richard II., it had been ordained that all woollen cloth brought for sale to London should be first lodged, under severe penalties for default, in the market of Blackwell Hall.

Shortly after the foundation of Christ's Hospital, the entire management of this market was vested in the Governors, and the revenues thence arising were applied towards the support of the institution, and the Queen's proclamation of 1580, forbidding any more buildings within two miles of the City, in consequence of the immense growth of the metropolis, directed forfeitures to go to the support of the City hospitals.

In 1685, the Court of Common Council made over "the rule, oversight, and government of cars, carts, carters, and carmen," to the Governors of Christ's Hospital, ordering that the "number of carts should not exceed 420 : to pay 17s. 4d. per annum each, and 20s. upon every admittance or alienation."

During the first forty-eight years of its foundation (1553—1600) the donations and legacies amounted to £9,828 9s. 8d., and it is stated by Mr. Hare, in his report, that the gifts of the twenty-four donors who made up this amount now give a rental of more than £13,000 a year to the Hospital.

In the first half of the seventeenth century, estates now worth about £4,000 a year had been devised, and in the second half of the same century (1650—1700), gifts of houses and lands, now of the value of about £15,000 a year, were added to the possessions of the Hospital, and so it has been growing, until at the present time the gross revenue of Christ's Hospital exceeds £70,000 a year.

We have not space to notice as they deserve the numerous benefactors of the institution; but we cannot omit mention of one munificent patron—Lady Ramsay—through whose great liberality boys were enabled to be sent to the University of Cambridge; and this lady may claim the honour of founding that purely classical part of the school which has been one of the grandest features of Christ's Hospital.

In the seventeenth and eighteenth centuries, one boy was sent annually to the university; but, owing to the great increase which has taken place in funds set apart for this particular purpose, as many as six or eight are now sent, and this special endowment fund is increasing in value so rapidly that before long Christ's Hospital will possess endowments for university education perhaps greater than those possessed by Eton or Winchester.

CHAPTER III.

SCHOOL BUILDINGS.

THE school buildings in London occupy about four acres. In the main they are of a modern character—only one cloister of the old Grey Friars Monastery now standing. "The Grey Friars Church," says Pennant, "was reckoned one of the most superb of the conventual establishments of London." In 1429, the immortal Whittington built the studious friars of Newgate Street a library, 129 feet long and 31 broad, with 28 desks and 8 double settles. In three years it was filled with books costing £556 10s., whereof Richard Whittington gave £400 and Dr. Thomas Winchilsey, one of the friars, the rest, adding an especial 100 marks for the writing out the works of D. Nicholas de Lyra, in two volumes to be trained there. Among the Royal contributors to the Grey Friars, we may mention Queen Margaret, second wife of Edward I., who gave in her lifetime 2,000 marks, and by will 100 marks, towards building a choir; John Britaine, Earl of Richmond, gave £300 towards the church building, besides jewels and ornaments; Mary, Countess of Pembroke, sent £70, and Gilbert de Clare, Earl of Gloucester, 20 great oak beams from his forest at Tunbridge and £20; the good Queen Philippa, wife of Edward III., £62; and Isabel, queen mother of Edward III., £70.

The Grey Friars churchyard was thought, in the Middle Ages, to be peculiarly free from incubi and flying demons of all sorts, and so it soon became a fashionable burying-place, and almost as popular as the great abbey, even with Royalty. Four queens lie there, among countless lords and ladies, brave knights and godly monks—Margaret, second wife of Edward I., and Isabella, the infamous wife and part murderess of Edward II., both, as we have before mentioned, benefactors to the Monastery; Joan, daughter of Edward II. and wife of David Bruce, King of Scotland; and, lastly, Isabella, wife of William, Baron Fitzwarren, titular Queen of Man. The English Queen Isabella, as if to propagate an eternal lie, was buried with the heart of her murdered husband on her breast. Her ghost, according to all true "Blues," still haunts the cloisters.

Here, also, rest other knights and ladies, almost equally illustrious by birth; among others, Isabella, daughter of Edward III., and wife of Ingelram de Courcy, Earl of Bedford; John Hastings, the young Earl of Pembroke, slain by accident at a Christmas tournament in Woodstock Park, 1389; John, Duke of Bourbon, one of the noble French prisoners taken at Agincourt, who had been a prisoner in the Tower eighteen years; Walter Blunt, Lord Mountjoy, Lord Treasurer to Edward IV., and the "gentle Mortimer," the wretched paramour of Queen Isabella, who was hung at Tyburn, and left two days withering on the gallows. Lastly, those two rapacious favourites of Richard II., Sir Robert Tresilian, Chief Justice of England, and Sir Nicholas Brembre, Lord Mayor of London, both hung at Tyburn. Tradition goes that they could not hang Tresilian till they had removed from his person certain magic images and the head of a devil.

The friars' churchyard seems also to have been fashionable with state criminals of the Middle Ages, for here also lies Sir John Mortimer, an unhappy Yorkist, hung, drawn, and quartered at Tyburn by the Lancastrian party in 1423 (the second year of the reign of the child-king, Henry VI.). To the same bourne also came a victim of Yorkist cruelty, Thomas Burdet, for speaking a few angry words about a favourite white buck which Edward IV. had carelessly killed. A murderess, too, lies here, a lady named Alice Hungerford, who, for murdering her husband in 1523, was carted to Tyburn, and there hung. All these ancient monuments and tombs were basely and stupidly sold, in 1545, by Sir Martin Bowes, Lord Mayor, for a poor fifty pounds. The great fire of 1666 destroyed the Grey Friars church, which Wren shortly afterwards rebuilt, a little further to the east, and in the old church perished the tomb of the beautiful Lady Venetia Digby, whom Ben Jonson celebrated, and who, it was absurdly supposed, perished from viper broth administered by her husband to heighten her beauty.

The fire of London destroyed a great portion of the school buildings, which were replaced about 1670. Extensive alterations also took place at the commencement of the present century, when it was resolved by the Governors to take down and rebuild on an extensive scale. For this purpose it was necessary to purchase and take in several adjoining premises, and an Act of Parliament was passed empowering the Governors to purchase certain premises in Little Britain, Newgate Street, and certain alleys and courts adjoining; and for the purpose of enlarging the hospital at Hertford, certain land contiguous thereto.

Under this Act great alterations and improvements were effected, and the means of carrying into execution their plans for rebuilding the Hospital in London were at length afforded by the completion of an exchange (highly beneficial to both parties) with the Governors of St. Bartholomew's Hospital in 1819. The new hall was commenced in 1825, and finished in 1829.

It was built by Mr. Thomas Souter from designs

of Mr. John Shaw, architect, and stands partly on the foundations of the ancient refectory, and partly on the site of the old City wall. The style is pure Gothic, and the southern or principal front is built of Portland stone with cloisters of Heytor granite, running beneath a portion of the dining-hall. Nine large and handsome windows occupy the entire front. On the ground storey are the Governors' room, the wardrobe, the buttery, and other offices; and the basement storey contains, besides cellars, &c., a spacious kitchen, 69 feet long by 33 feet wide, supported by massive granite pillars. The hall itself, with its lobby and organ-gallery, occupies the entire upper storey, which is 187 feet long, 51½ feet wide, and 46½ feet high. It was at one time (and perhaps still is) famous for its rats, who, attracted by the crumbs and fragments of food, foraged about after dark in hundreds. It used to be the peculiar pride of an old "Blue" to catch these rats with his hands only, traps being considered cowardly aids to humanity and unworthy of the Hospital. The old dusty picture-frames are favourite terraces for these vermin.

The two famous pictures in the hall—neither of them of much real merit, but valuable for their portraits—are those of Edward VI. renewing his father's gift of the Hospital, and of St. Thomas and Bridewell, to the City, falsely ascribed to Holbein, who died seven or eight years before it took place; and "sprawling" Verrio's picture of James II. receiving an audience of Christ's Hospital boys and girls. The pseudo-Holbein and the painting by Verrio are both well described by Malcolm. The so-called Holbein "adorns the west wall, and is placed near the entrance, at the north end of the hall. The king is seated on a throne, elevated on two steps, with two very clumsy brackets for arms, on which are fanciful pilasters, adorned with carving, and an arch; on the left pilaster, a crowned lion holding a shield, with the letter 'E'; a dragon on the other has another inscribed 'R.' Two angels, reclining on the arch, support the arms of England. The hall of audience is represented as paved with black and white marble; the windows are angular, with niches between each. As there are statues in only two of those, it seems to confirm the idea that it is an exact resemblance of the royal apartment.

"The artist has bestowed his whole attention on the young monarch, whose attitude is easy, natural, and dignified. He presents the deed of gift with his right hand, and holds the sceptre in his left. The scarlet robe is embroidered, and lined with ermine, and the folds are correctly and minutely finished. An unavoidable circumstance injures the effect of this picture, which is the diminutive stature of the infant-king, who shrinks into a dwarf, compared with his full-grown courtiers; unfortunately, reversing the necessary rule of giving most dignity and consequence to the principal person in the piece.

"The chancellor holds the seal over his crossed arms at the king's right hand. This officer and three others are the only standing figures. Ridley kneels at the foot of the throne, and shows his face in profile with uplifted hands. On the right are the Mayor and Aldermen, in scarlet robes, kneeling. Much cannot be said in praise of those worthies. The members of the Common Council, &c., on the other side, are grouped with more skill, and the action is more varied. The heads of the spectators are generally full of anxious attention.

"But five of twenty-eight children who are introduced in the foreground turn towards the king; the remainder look out of the picture. The matron on the girls' side (if a portrait) was chosen for her mental and not her personal qualifications. Such are the merits and defects of this celebrated painting. which, though infinitely inferior to many of Holbein's Dutch and Italian contemporaries, is a valuable, and in many respects an excellent, historic composition.

"Verrio's enormous picture" of James II. and the Blue-Coat children "must originally have been in three parts: the centre on the end wall, and the two others on the adjoining sides. Placed thus, the perspective of the depths of the arches would have been right; as it is at present, extended on one plane, they are exactly the reverse. The audience-chamber is of the Ionic order, with twenty pilasters, and their entablatures and arches. The passage, seen through those, has an intersected arched ceiling. The king sits in the centre of the painting, on a throne of crimson damask, with the royal arms embroidered on the drapery of the canopy, the front of which is of fringed white cloth of gold. The footstool is of purple cloth of gold, and the steps of the throne are covered by a rich Turkey carpet, not remarkably well-painted. The king holds a scroll in his left hand, extends the right, and seems to address a person immediately before him. The position of his body and the foreshortened arm are excellent, and the lace and drapery are finely drawn and coloured. On the sides of the throne are two circular portraits.

"The painter has committed a strange error in turning the king's face from the Lord Mayor, who points in vain to an extended map, a globe, and all the kneeling figures, exulting in the progress of their forty boys in the mathematics, who are busily employed in producing their cases and definitions. Neither in such an attitude could the king observe fourteen kneeling girls, though their faces and persons are handsome and graceful, and the matron and her assistant seem eager to place them in the monarch's view. Verrio has stationed himself at the extreme end of the picture, and his expression appears to inquire the spectators' opinion of his performance. On the opposite side a yeoman of the guard clears the way for some person, and a female seems alarmed at his violence, but a full-dressed youth before him looks out of the picture with the utmost indifference. There is one excellent head which speaks earnestly to a boy. Another figure, probably the master or steward, pulls a youth's hair with marks of anger. Several lords-in-waiting are correct and good figures.

"At the upper end of the room, and on the same west wall, is a large whole-length of Charles II. descending from his throne, a curtain from which is turned round a pillar. The king holds his robe with his right hand, and points with the left to a globe and mathematical instruments."

On the south side of the entrance from Little Britain is the treasurer's house, and the other houses in this playground are occupied by the matron, masters, and beadles. Proceeding in an easterly direction leads to the south-east entrance from Butcher Hall Lane, Newgate Street, and in this space (which is called the counting-house yard) stands the counting-house, and several other houses, which are inhabited by the clerks and some of the masters. The treasurer has also a back entrance to his house, at the end of the counting-house, and his garden runs at the back of all the houses on the east side of this yard. The opposite building is occupied by the boys, and in a niche in the centre, fronting the door of the counting-house, is a statue of King Edward (considered the most perfect one), which represents his majesty, who stands on a black marble slab, in the act of delivering the charter.

The mathematical school is over the old west

entrance, now closed up, and was built by Wren, with a ward for the foundation boys over it. A robed statue of Charles II., dated 1672, stands over the gateway. The entrance leads to the north-west corner of the cloisters, which form the four shady sides of the garden playground, and have porticoes, with Gothic arches all round. The walls are supported by abutments of the old priory. Wren repaired the cloisters, which are useful to the young blue monks for play and promenade in wet weather.

The boys have three playgrounds, the hall play-ground, the Garden—so called from its having been " the garden " adjoining the monastery—and "The Ditch," one of the town ditches, now a sewer, running through this portion of the property.

CHAPTER IV.

PECULIAR BEQUESTS.

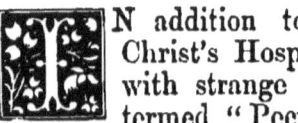N addition to many munificent donations, Christ's Hospital has been richly endowed with strange bequests, with what may be termed "Peculiarity with a purpose," or " Benevolence with a twist." To instance a few only :—

Robert Hilson, citizen and mercer, in 1582, gave to the Governors of Christ's Hospital for ever the sum of £10 14s. 8d. "towards the relief of the poor children in the said Hospital, towards providing black caps for them; requiring that the said poor children, or the biggest sort of them, might ever after wear round black caps, as they used to wear."

Robert Symonds, also a citizen and mercer, in 1586, gave the sum of 3s. 4d. a year to be expended in raisins to be distributed on Good Friday to sixty Blue-Coat boys, who should on the morning of that day, every year, come to the church of All Saints* in Lumber Street, and there in the said church and chancel receive the same, together with the small sum of one penny, thoughtfully provided by Peter Symonds, to help the raisins down.

This good man was dreadfully afraid that his munificence might not be appreciated, for his will states his gift may possibly be thought very frivolous, "yet my mind and meaning being hidden, may notwithstanding be performed."

It is perhaps needless to add that the donor's "mind and meaning" remain hidden to this day, but Peter Symonds has received the while a very cheap advertisement, for the Blue-Coat boys have made pilgrimage to Lumber Street for nearly 300 years —and still they go—and their going has given rise to a doggerel familiar to all "Old Blues":

> "Come, little Blue-Coat boy, come, come, come,
> Sing for a penny, and chant for a plum."

A more thoughtful and acceptable donor now appears in the person of William Mascall, another citizen and mercer, who in 1608 gave the sum of £8 10s. "to be bestowed on the children of the said hospital at Michaelmas and Midsummer, in providing for them a dinner or supper of roast beef or mutton, allowing £4 5s. for each meal."

It does not appear at what hour Blue-Coat boys in the reign of the first James had their supper and went to bed, but it does occur to one that if William Mascall had concentrated all his benevolence on dinner, it might have accorded more with dietetics; but we have this consolation, that Mr. William Mascall in his kindness did not insist upon pork!

---

* All Hallows, Lombard Street.

The next donor is a merchant-tailor, Robert Dow by name, who "had a grateful commiseration for the poor children, and a desire to encourage skilful teachers to do their best endeavours in the instructing of the said poor children in the heavenly science of music," and he gave the sum of £20 per year for carrying out his very laudable desire, and further, "for comforting and cherishing the said poor children," Robert Dow also left the sum of 40s. to be laid out annually in fuel in June or July, to be then deposited in the school cellars for winter's use; and he further directed that 6d. should be expended annually upon each boy for a pair of gloves, and 8d. was ordered to be expended upon gloves for the master.

In 1612, William Stoddard, skinner, by whose gift ten poor children of freemen of the Skinners' Company are educated in Christ's Hospital, gave the sum of £4 yearly to be expended in providing two dinners for the children, one on New Year's Day, and the other on Candlemas Day.

In 1608, Mr. Mascall had estimated the boys' dinner to cost £4 5s., so that it is somewhat difficult to understand how four years later it could only have cost £2. Perhaps Mr. Stoddard's prophetic eye caught a glimpse of Australian meat!

Mr. Stoddard, for reasons which do not appear, ordered his ten boys to wear green caps and green facings on the coats; but the Governors, who never had anything green about them, have done Mr. Stoddard a service by refusing to give his ten boys this green distinction.

In 1625 James Wood, of London, bowyer, gave a freehold messuage to the Hospital on condition that yearly on Thursday after St. James's Day, the poor children should have "good and wholesome flesh, roasted for them."

Sir John Gayer's gift (1641) is rather peculiar.

For seven years the annual sum bequeathed (£25) is ordered to be spent in premiums in the " putting out " of children, but in every eighth year the children are to have a dinner of roast beef, " or other cates; " two scholars proceeding to the University are to be rewarded with £5 each; a sermon is to be preached, for which 30s. is allowed, and before the sermon the Governors are to be fortified with a " collation; " and sums of money varying from 2s. to 20s. are to be given to the servants of the Hospital. In short, in every eighth year, everybody was to be made comfortable all round.

In 1615, Randolph Wooley, merchant-tailor, gave 50s. for a dinner for the children on Easter-day, and; in 1619, we come upon the first of a long list of sermon bequests, and this first sermon is very properly ordered to be preached not *to* the boys, but *at* the Governors, who are enjoined to proceed to church " in a grave manner."

John Bancks, at whose instigation the sermon is preached, was good enough to give directions that it should be over by ten o'clock, in order that six of the Governors, with the treasurer, preacher, schoolmaster, and usher, might dine together afterwards, and drink to the memory of John Bancks, citizen and mercer of London.

The sermon is still preached annually on St. Matthew's Day, by a scholar and exhibitioner of the school at one of the universities.

In 1651, George Dunn, having a desire that the Blue-Coat boys should have the Gunpowder Plot in annual remembrance, resolved, so far as £3 worth of roast beef would do it, that his purpose should be accomplished; and for more than two centuries the boys have blessed the arch conspirator of that plot as no mean benefactor; and in the following year John Babington gave the sum of 40s. for ever, to be laid out in roast meat for the boys, to be by them digested as "near the time of my burial as may be."

About this time (1654), Rowland Wilson gave the interest on £100 to be expended in roast meat for the boys on St. Andrew's Day. After this run of roast meat, Richard Young, in 1661, gives us an agreeable change. This worthy was an author, with a soul above mutton. I remember when a boy I had some "night thoughts," which were not by Young, for the thoughts of this worthy were no doubt meant to be considered by the boys by day.

He was the author of three works entitled respectively—"A short and sure way to Grace and Salvation;" "The Heart's Index, or Self Knowledge;" "A serious and pathetical description of Heaven and Hell."

Two thousand copies were ordered to be printed for the boys, and two thousand were to be supplied yearly to the Chamberlain of the City.

They were last printed in 1776, and we regret to say that the Chamberlain has only once applied to the school authorities for them, and that a large stock remains on hand.

In 1663, Thomas Barnes left £4 a-year to be laid out in roasted beef or mutton on every 5th of November, and 20s. yearly for a sermon on the 17th of November, that being Queen Elizabeth's coronation day, and £10 yearly for the governors who attended the service.

In 1669 Edward Arris left an annual sum of £6 to be expended in purchasing white gloves and a paper with the words

"He is risen"

upon it, to be worn by the boys at Easter. The "Risens," as we used to call them, are still worn, and

I regret to say that youthful ardour has invented a doggerel as follows :—

> "He is risen—He is risen,
> Send the wretched Jews to prison."

By will dated 1670, William Pennoyer gave the sum of £50 for ever to the authorities, £40 of which was ordered to be expended in placing out eight poor children ; 40s. for eight Bibles for the said children ; 40s. yearly to buy the president a pair of gloves (I don't know whether his Royal Highness the Duke of Cambridge wears his on state occasions) ; £4 yearly to the treasurer for his care and pains ; and 40s. yearly to the clerk for keeping the accounts, and for reading, annually, so much of Mr. Pennoyer's will as relates to the legacy.

Eight years later, 1678, the Hospital found a munificent patron in Thomas Stretchley ; for, though some directions in his will are peculiar, his legacy is decidedly substantial, for he left a sum of money sufficient to purchase land in England to the annual value of £380.

Out of this sum he gave £10 to (1st), "Ten poor ministers of honest lives and conversation above sixty years of age." (2nd), "Ten poor widows of lawful ministers about fifty years of age." (3rd) "Five prisons—viz., Ludgate, Newgate, the Compter in Wood Street, the Compter in the Poultry, and the Fleet ; the £10 to be enjoyed by the ministers, widows, and prisoners every third year."

With respect to the prisoners the money is ordered to be expended upon " the poorest of them, such as are usually in the holes of the said prisons ;" and the good man also ordered £4 more to be annually expended in releasing or buying out of prison two male or female prisoners ; then we have 25s. for a sermon to the governors of Christ's Hospital, and a sum of money sufficient to buy sixty leathern caps and sixty pairs of woollen " mittings," to be worn by the weakest or sickest sort of children resident within the school.

In 1684, Sir John Frederick, amongst other gifts, left £100 to be invested in the purchase of land, of the annual value of £5, to be spent at the half-yearly examinations in ale, cake, and wine, for the governors; and an annual dinner of roast beef or mutton on St. Matthew's Day, was given by Sir John Johnson in 1692.

In 1699, John Oliver, master mason to His Majesty, did a sensible thing in providing a dinner of roast beef for the boys on Christmas Day; and in 1701, Charles Adams left the sum of £100 to be invested for the purchase of "The Whole Duty of Man," which, oddly enough, is ordered to be given to young persons of either sex on leaving the school. And in 1707, Mary Plumb gave the interest of £100 for the purchase of boiled legs of pork for the children on the 22nd February in each year; and in 1725, Sir George Mertins, Knight and Alderman of London, evidently anxious that the boys should have Queen Anne in daily and nightly remembrance, ordered a sum of money to be annually laid out in legs and shoulders of veal, to be had by the boys on Queen Anne's birthday.

We have not been able to understand how veal and Queen Anne became connected, but it would certainly appear from numerous legacies that the only way known to commemorate the Queen's virtues about this time consisted in swallowing an inordinate quantity of veal; for in 1731, another worthy, Samuel Davenport, left £250 for the purchase of legs and shoulders of veal for a dinner for the boys on the anniversary of Queen Anne's accession, and he also gave a picture of Queen Anne to the governors, and the sum of five guineas to be expended in purchasing any history of that Queen, when the governors were satisfied it was well done; and in 1733, Sarah Lorrain left the poor boys another dinner of veal on every 1st of August; and in 1748, yet another dinner of meat was provided for the boys by Benjamin Johnson, of Twickenham, on every 12th day of October, that being the birthday of King Edward VI.

An interesting bequest is that of Mr. St. Amand, who left the residue of his estate to the governors, and at no period have the authorities had less than £8,000 invested in the Three per Cents., arising from his legacy.

Mr. St. Amand gave to the treasurer and governors of Christ's Hospital "the original portrait of his grandfather, John St. Amand," but this portrait is believed to be that of the Pretender, of whom the donor was an adherent.

With respect to the present pecuniary position of the Hospital, I may mention that in consequence of the recent action of the Endowed Schools Commissioners, the annual revenue from Donation Governors, which was formerly about £5,000 a year, has considerably fallen off, to about £2,000 a year, and very recently the authorities have had to sell out a portion of stock in order to meet current expenses.

CHAPTER V.

FAMOUS BLUES.

THE after career of the scholars is the surest test of the efficiency of a public school—of the attainment of the objects for which an institution, such as Christ's Hospital, is founded. And the test, to be really valuable, must

be applied in two ways. In the first place, we ask whether men of marked distinction have been educated on the foundation ; in the second place, we desire to know—and this is probably of more importance, as showing the broad and general results of the instruction imparted—whether the great body of the pupils have, after leaving school, met with a fair amount of success in fighting the battle of life.

That both these proofs of efficiency have been amply afforded by the Blue-Coat School may be unhesitatingly affirmed on the authority of facts, in all cases well ascertained, in many cases perfectly notorious.

It must not be expected, however, that a foundation like Christ's Hospital can have so many really great names associated with it as such schools as Eton, Harrow, and Rugby—schools to which, as a rule, only the children of the wealthiest and most cultured classes are sent, and whence the scholars commonly proceed to the army or navy; or to the universities, there to go through a further course of instruction before entering on a professional or political career.

But, though used as an educational institution for children destined, for the most part, to trades or to mercantile pursuits, the Blue-Coat School can boast a long array of men of learning, eminence, and distinguished ability; while some, whose names will never be forgotten as long as the rich and ripe literature of England survives, were educated on the foundation.

Of the more eminent scholars—of the truly famous Blues—we shall speak at some length presently; in the meanwhile, we may notice briefly those who have distinguished themselves in a lesser, but still in a highly respectable degree.

"During the last twenty-two years," it was stated in evidence before the Charity Commission Inquiry in

1865, "owing to largely increased exhibition funds being at the disposal of the governors, they have been able to send three, four, and latterly five Grecians annually to the universities. Of the Grecians preferred to college in the course of the last thirty years (to connect with the termination of the Rev. William Trollope's list), nineteen or twenty have been in the list of Wranglers, and have taken the second, fourth, eighth, tenth, twelfth, and various lower places, besides two who were Double First-Class men; ten others have been in the First Class in Classics, eleven have become Fellows, one was first in Classics and First Chancellor's Medallist, after carrying off a large (perhaps unprecedented) number of previous distinctions, and at an early age was appointed to the Regius Chair of Civil Law at Cambridge, then to that of Reader in Civil Law at the Inner Temple, and is now the Legal Member of the Supreme Council in India."

The witness goes on to give particulars as to the subsequent careers of the successful "Blues" mentioned in the above list, and points out that some are fellows and tutors of their colleges; that six are head masters of public schools; several are barristers; some are clergymen; and one holds a high judicial appointment in India. "Several of the Grecians," says the witness, "who have left within the period now referred to, have applied themselves to literature, and several have died; but rare indeed have been the instances of Grecians who are known to have done otherwise than well."

Of former naval or royal mathematical boys, the same unimpeachable authority tells us—we must bear in mind that he is speaking of 1865—that several held high rank in the royal navy, including a rear-admiral and a captain, C.B.; one, a retired captain in the army, and one who was in command of a merchant ship belonging to the late East India Company, were governors of the Hospital, and many others were in commands of some importance in China, India, and elsewhere.

"Since 1858," the witness goes on to say, "owing to the facilities afforded by the Supplemental Charter granted by her present Majesty, many of the royal mathematical boys have entered the royal navy, either as naval cadets or as masters' or clerks' assistants, and already several have been mentioned with great commendation.

"It may be added, on the authority of one of the mathematical masters, that those who have joined the navy have generally taken high places in the examinations; of the nine who entered as naval cadets, five passed either in the preliminary or final examination, and five have received first-class certificates. Of the sixteen who entered as clerks' or masters' assistants, six have taken the first place. One after leaving school obtained a commission in the Royal Marines, and passed first. Of the whole number only two or three have been lower than sixth in any examination. Others have entered the Peninsular and Oriental and other companies' services, as well as many of the best private services connected with the port of London. There is every reason for believing that these boys, scattered over the world, and therefore generally less heard of than the Grecians, do credit to their old school, and look back to it with affection and good feeling."

Of the general mass of boys who leave the Hospital in the ordinary way at fifteen years of age, or thereabouts, we are told that "they are to be found in almost every rank of society, and in nearly every profession, trade, and class of employment. Comparatively few of them are known to be in the law, although those few include a serjeant-at-law, and a barrister and six or eight solicitors, the cost of the stamp on the articles, added to the premium required, being commonly beyond the means of the boys' parents or friends. The same observation may be made in reference to the profession of architects, although here one name of eminence and several of high respectability can be mentioned, and to some extent it holds also with regard to civil engineers, amongst whom, however, one well-known name is that of a Blue. A considerable number of Blues are known to be in the medical profession, and names of great respectability and even eminence (including one of the serjeant surgeons to the Queen) can be mentioned amongst them. Several, not to say many, are clergymen, having worked through the universities without the Hospital's exhibitions, and of these one is now a Canon of St. Paul's, and one a Canon and Archdeacon of Winchester; another was Fellow and Mathematical Lecturer of his college, and several have done very well indeed. The name of the late Rev. Hartwell Horne, a former deputy Grecian, must ever be mentioned with respect as one of the most learned and distinguished amongst Blues. One (now deceased) of such clergymen not 'Grecians' was lately a governor of the Hospital, and another was, until his recent resignation, master of one of the city companies' schools. It is thought that few old Blues become farmers, but many of them are to be found in the city as thriving merchants; some are successful stock-brokers, others are largely engaged in trade as colonial or other brokers, or as wholesale dealers; many are retail tradesmen. A well-known old Blue and governor of the Hospital has lately retired from partnership in a publishing firm of eminence second to none, and another is now a partner in the same firm and a governor also; two are city deputies, and several, during the last few years, have been members of the Common Council. A well-known late town-clerk of London was a Blue, and the present chief clerk to the Chamberlain and several other civic officials were Blues. A Lord Mayor of rather more than twenty years since was a former Blue. In the Bank of England, one or more Blues may be found in almost every office, and in the large joint-stock banks, as well as in the private banks, there are a considerable number of them, and in several instances they hold high positions. The like may be said of the insurance offices, the docks, and other large mercantile establishments.

"Amongst government officials to whom allusion may be made as 'old Blues,' may be mentioned the present secretary, as well as the comptroller-general of the Customs, the receiver or accountant-general of the Post Office, the accountants at the Charity Commission and Inclosure Commission, besides one or more Blues in the Admiralty, the Treasury, the War Office, the Inland Revenue, the India Office, Queen Anne's Bounty, and various other public departments, one being also a C.B.

"It is understood that not many Blues are in the army, the expense of the necessary further education on leaving the Hospital at fifteen years of age, coupled with the cost of the commission and the outfit, being generally beyond the means of the parents or immediate relatives; nevertheless, in the late East Indian army, two (one of whom is deceased) are known to have attained the rank of major-general, and several others have held, and some continue to hold, good rank in the army in India. A Blue, now a governor, was an assistant-surgeon on board one of the ships engaged in the siege of Acre; another was surgeon on board the *Tiger*, and was taken prisoner in the Crimean war; and another young man, F.R.C.S., fell a victim to disease at Scutari after accompanying wounded men from Balaklava."

The first "Blue" of any eminence, Edmund Campian, the celebrated Jesuit, came to an untimely and ignominious end. After living for some years as Professor of Rhetoric at a catholic college at Prague, he returned to England with the view of bringing back the wavering and the lukewarm to their old allegiance to the Romish Church. This was an interference with the work of the Reformation which Queen Elizabeth was by no means disposed to tolerate, and Campian being unearthed by the emissaries of Walsingham, then Secretary of State, was hanged at Tyburn in 1581. Camden, the antiquary, who is believed to have been also a "Blue," though on this point there is considerable doubt, had a much happier fate. He received an appointment in the Heralds' College, founded a history lecture at Oxford, and died in 1623, in his house at Chiselhurst, in Kent —a mansion recently occupied by the ex-Emperor, Napoleon III. Joshua Barnes, at one time Greek Professor at Cambridge, was however unquestionably a Blue-Coat boy, and gained no little distinction from his editions of Homer and Anacreon. Another "Blue" of renown was Jeremiah Markland, a learned scholar and critic who defended Addison's character against Pope's satire. Amongst others we may mention Richardson the novelist; and, coming to a later period, George Dyer, Val Le Grice, and James White, all men of more or less ability, but who will be remembered chiefly as friends of Charles Lamb. Meyer, a portrait painter of some celebrity in his day, and the Rev. Thomas Mitchell, one of the best translators of and commentators upon the plays of Aristophanes, were also "Blues," and reflected no little lustre on the institution in which they received their education.

In diplomacy the school can claim, in times past, Sir Edward Thornton; in medicine we may point to

Dr. Irwin, once a famous physician, and for some time President of the College of Physicians.

Some of the highest offices in the Church of England have been filled by clergymen who were once "Blues." The famous Bishop Stillingfleet, Dr. Middleton, the first Bishop of Calcutta, who died in 1822, and the Rev. Rowley Hill, M.A., the newly appointed Bishop of Sodor and Man, were all educated on the foundation of Christ's Hospital, and proceeded thence to one or other of the universities. It may be interesting to mention, of the last-named prelate, that he is still in the prime of his age, having passed out of the school as a Grecian in 1855, and at the time of his nomination to the bishopric was vicar of Sheffield, which living he has held since 1873.

But of all the "old Blues" who have attained distinction, three stand head and shoulders above their brethren. Leigh Hunt, Charles Lamb, and—greatest of the three—Samuel Taylor Coleridge, are names that the world will not readily let die. The two latter were contemporaries—Leigh Hunt some years their junior. The friendship which sprang up between Lamb and Coleridge in their youth, a friendship always intimate and tender, was never interrupted by the jealousies or aberrations of genius, and ended only with life; it was a love founded, perhaps, on intellectual appreciation, but nourished by mutual regard and by the subtle sympathy which sometimes links together natures that at first sight seem most dissimilar, and to have no common bond of union. One can imagine Lamb, the quiet, shy, timid schoolboy, listening in rapt admiration to the fascinating fluency of speech, and marvelling at the rich abundance of thought, for which Coleridge was distinguished even in his early youth; but it shows a more rare and delicate appreciation of character on the part of Coleridge that he should have perceived instinctively the genius that lay hidden under the unpromising exterior, the reserved habits, and the retiring disposition of the future author of the "Essays of Elia." But between the two schoolfellows, so richly and yet so differently endowed, from whatever cause it may have originated, a warm and ardent friendship, a true soul companionship, always subsisted. Lamb's was the more delicate and tremblingly sensitive, Coleridge's the fuller and the grander nature; and, remembering this, there seems to be something almost idyllic in the constancy of their mutual attachment, especially when we consider the proverbial irritability of authors, and that these men each took a place in the foremost ranks of literature, even in an age of literary giants. Coleridge and Lamb are as real to us as Dr. Johnson himself when looked at through the medium of Boswell's wonderful biography. Whether in the cloisters of Christ's Hospital, or, later on, at their convivial gatherings, or in their home lives— lives as different as their diverse natures, yet alike very touching, true, and tender, we see them "in their habits as they lived"—Charles, awkward in manner, hesitating in speech, yet always cordial and sweetly sympathetic; his friend, ready, confident, full to overflowing with learning, and continually pouring forth poetry and metaphysics with a copious eloquence at once unsurpassed and unsurpassable.

Of Coleridge at school Charles Lamb says:— "Come back into memory, like as thou wert in the dayspring of thy fancies, with hope, like a fiery column, before thee—the dark pillar not yet turned —Samuel Taylor Coleridge, logician, metaphysician, bard! How have I seen the casual passer through the cloisters stand still, entranced with admiration (while he weighed the disproportion between the *speech* and the *garb* of the young Mirandula), to hear thee unfold, in thy deep and sweet intonations, the mysteries of Jamblichus or Plotinus (for even in those years thou waxedest not pale at such philosophic draughts), or reciting Homer in his Greek, or Pindar, while the walls of the old Grey Friars re-echoed to the accents of the *inspired charity-boy!* Many were the 'wit-combats' (to dally awhile with the words of old Fuller) between him and C. V. Le Grice, 'which, too, I behold, like a Spanish great galleon and an English man-of-war. Master Coleridge, like the former, was built far higher in learning, solid, but slow in his performances. C. V. L., with the English man-of-war, lesser in bulk, but lighter in sailing could turn with all tides, tack about, and take advantage of all winds, by the quickness of his wit and invention."

Referring to Charles Lamb, Leigh Hunt says:— "I have spoken of the distinguished individuals bred at Christ's Hospital, including Coleridge and Lamb, who left the school not long before I entered it. Coleridge I never saw till he was old. Lamb I recollect coming to see the boys, with a pensive, brown, handsome, and kindly face, and a gait advancing with a motion from side to side, between involuntary consciousness and attempted ease. His brown complexion may have been owing to a visit in the country; his air of uneasiness, to a great burden of sorrow. He dressed with a quaker-like plainness. I did not know him as Lamb; I took him for a Mr. 'Guy,' having heard somebody address him by that appellative, I suppose in jest."

Although Leigh Hunt cannot be considered the equal of either of the two distinguished "Blues" we have just named, he was undeniably a man of very versatile ability, and of talent so conspicuous and in many respects so remarkable that it hardly, if at all, falls short of genius. His reputation will always be considerable of its kind, and in an age less affluent in literature of the highest class, it might even have been commanding. One of Leigh Hunt's contemporaries, Thomas Barnes, formerly editor of the *Times*, was also educated at Christ's Hospital, and of him, Hunt says, that no man, if he had cared for it, could have been more certain of distinction.

When the great cause of metropolitan education required organising, an old "Blue," Mr. Croad, was selected to steer the craft through its difficult, tortuous, and uncertain navigation; and Mr. Scudamore, another old "Blue," was, some time since, specially appointed to organise the postal arrangements of Turkey. Sir H. Sumner Maine, the distinguished author, and late a member of the Council of India; Sir Henry Cole, of South Kensington celebrity; Peter Cunningham, author and critic; the late Canon Dale; Richard Thornton, the well-known millionaire; the late Head Master of the London School, the Rev. G. C. Bell, a Grecian some five and twenty years ago, and a double first class man at Oxford, and now Head Master at Marlborough; Dr. Haig Brown, of the Charterhouse; and many others too numerous to mention, now hold high and responsible positions at the universities, public schools, and other places of learning. Sir Thomas Duffus Hardy, of the Public Record Office, was also educated in the Blue-Coat School.

Many pages, indeed even a goodly volume, might be filled with interesting anecdotes of eminent men who were once scholars at Christ's Hospital; but we must content ourselves with adding to what we have already said, that nearly all the Grecians sent up to the universities have taken a creditable, and many, as we have seen, a distinguished, place in the world. Of late years the benefits of a college education have been conferred on a far greater number of the scholars than was formerly the case, and the institution has thus been made more largely useful; while, there is every reason to believe, from the experience of the past, that as the means at their disposal increase, the authorities will afford to still greater numbers the opportunity of obtaining the highest kind of culture. In the course of the first two centuries of its existence, speaking roughly, or up to the year 1760, the Hospital only sent 155 students to the great seats of learning; in the next 82 years, 104 were sent; while in the 33 years between 1842 and 1875 the number amounted to 164, or, as nearly as possible, to an average of five per annum.

CHAPTER VI.

LIFE AT HERTFORD.

IN the year 1843, my grandfather received an intimation from one of the city aldermen that a presentation to Christ's Hospital was at his disposal, and in due course I presented myself at the counting-house in Newgate Street, to undergo the usual medical examination. The school authorities are very strict in this preliminary examination, and very properly so, too, for in the squad of fifteen, which passed under the doctor's eye when I was examined, one boy had actually been brought to the school in an advanced stage of scarlet fever! He was, of course, sent back to his parents, and as I never saw the boy afterwards, I am sadly afraid he did not recover in time to make use of the presentation, if indeed he recovered at all. After the examination, our friends were ordered to bring us again the next day for good. I say for good, for it seemed to many a fond parent that an eternity was about to separate them from their darling. One poor boy whose appearance betokened a "Parochial dragging-up," was brought to the school by a veritable "Bumble." His youthful hose, a world too wide for his shrunk shank, told us at once that he was an inferior animal, and so we were not long in making him understand his proper position. With respect to the others, as they came from various strata of the great middle class, and belonged to parents more or less wealthy,—there was nothing particularly striking or *outré* about their appearance. The boys are sent immediately on admission to the preparatory school at Hertford, and the beadle from that establishment was in attendance to escort us thither. I shall never forget the commanding presence and business-like manner of old C——. "Now Buggins, Spanker, Cauker, Smallbones, Squills, &c., this way. Make haste and change your clothes, for I can't be kept here all day!" He had actually learnt all our names in about five minutes, and, for aught I know to the contrary, had posted himself up in our birth, parentage, &c.

"The fond, attentive gaze of young astonishment" was shivered in a moment into ten thousand fragments! For the first time in life I had a severe attack of "Beadle on the brain." I began to feel that I was under a beadle despotism, and it took me eight years to recover from it.

We got into our new clothes as best we could, and I can well remember the pride with which I stepped forth, giving no thought to the discarded integuments, a full-blown "Blue." I had now blossomed into breeches, and had become a member of that large and respectable household—the CRUG FAMILY. It was a touching scene, to witness the pride with which some of the boys were regarded as they emerged from the wardrobe. The peculiar, quaint, and distinctive dress may have something of the touch of charity about it, but what a noble charity after all! A mother's feelings on parting with her boy has thus been described in a poem on Christ's Hospital :—

> "Mark now the stripling, his first thought employ,
> On his new livery as a Blue-Coat boy!
> Matilda views him with a mother's eyes,
> Joys that he stays—and yet to leave him, sighs,
> 'Till he, of his new privileges proud,
> Flies from her arms, and joins the sportive crowd.
> Then grateful, sorrowful, she wends her way,
> Cheer'd with hope's vision of a future day,
> Which gilds the evening of her life and joy,
> When he, whom she now leaves a helpless boy,
> Mature in years and virtues shall arise,
> To soothe the cares of age, and close her peaceful eyes."

And now before we start on our way to Hertford, let us give a few particulars as to the regulations for admission to the school. In the first place the children were required to be between eight and eleven years of age, though now it is limited to eight and ten. Their heads must be free from ——they must, also, be free from disease, as well as from any physical defect, which would render them unable to take care of themselves, and their parents must be without adequate means to educate and maintain them, and, as a matter of course, the children must not have any means of their own. The parents of the boy were compelled to make a written statement, showing their amount of income, with particulars of its source, the total number of children in the family, and how many of them were still young and dependent. Certificates of the parents' marriage, and of the child's birth and baptism, were in all cases produced before admission. All boys were required, as a preliminary to admission, to pass an examination as to their previous attainments. Boys between eight and nine years of age were expected to be able to read with facility any elementary book, to write legibly, and to say the multiplication table. Between nine and ten, in addition to the above, to be able to spell fairly from dictation, and to work the four simple rules of arithmetic; between ten and eleven, in addition to the above subjects, to have a fair knowledge of the compound rules of arithmetic, and the Latin accidence.

We must now join our little party, which is ready to proceed on its way. A coach was in readiness at Bishopsgate-street, at a well-known hostelry, to convey us to our destination. Under ordinary circumstances the ride to Hertford by coach (for it was in the pre-railway days) would no doubt have been an enjoyable excursion, but my surroundings on that memorable morning were by no means of an ordinary character. In the first place, the weather was unfavourable in the extreme (for it was in the dreary month of November), and consequently the whole of us, fourteen in number, were packed inside the coach, jammed as closely together as sardines in a tin box. The boys, however, only resembled those oily little customers in one respect—they could each a tale unfold, and wonderful, indeed, were the stories told by some of the more loquacious youngsters, of the wealth of their parents, and the grandeur of the homes they were leaving behind. Amidst all the youthful merry-making and exuberant spirits, however, one boy in a remote corner of the coach had been quietly emptying his capacious pocket of its varied contents, so that his stomach soon answered aptly enough to the lines of Pope—

"The stomach crammed from every dish,
A tomb of boiled and roast, and flesh and fish,
Where bile and wind, and phlegm and acid jar,
And all the boy is one intestine war."

It would not have concerned us much if the war

had been confined to the boy's own dominions, but like other great conquerors, he must needs carry the strife into other countries, and so by the time we reached our destination every one of us bore an outward and visible sign of the inward and revolutionary upheaving which had taken place. It was with no slight feeling of relief that we were released from our confinement, and allowed once more to breathe the pure and invigorating air. Our arrival had been anxiously looked forward to by the inmates of the school, who crowded round us, and took stock of our appearance, in remarks by no means flattering, somewhat after the manner of the dear creatures on Ramsgate Pier, on the arrival of the husbands' boat after a severe storm, with its usual concomitants!

We soon settled down to our respective dormitories, after having been sent to the nurse for "our blacking and brushes," and made the usual demand to have our mouths measured for spoons. Soon after my admission, the nurse of my ward had been compelled to leave the school on account of ill health, and a couple of days elapsed before her successor put in an appearance. In the interregnum the boys ran wild. During the night our exuberant spirits found full vent. There are two dormitories to each ward, the chamber and the attic. I was an inmate of the lower room, "the chamber," and while labouring under the impression that the "steward" was oblivious of school doings, the occupants of the two rooms marshalled themselves in warlike array. It was arranged that the attic occupants were to take possession of the stairs which led from the lower to the upper regions, while we of the lower chamber were to assault and carry by storm the defended position.

Arming ourselves with girdles, bolsters, and every available weapon of an offensive description, we gallantly rushed to the attack. Long and furious was the conflict, and assaults gallantly made were as gallantly repulsed, and many a warrior who went into action with his *robe de chambre*, returned from the attack in the primitive state of our first parents. For a long time the fortunes of the contending parties varied—now attacked, now attacking—the defenders stubbornly held their ground, and swollen faces and bloody noses were the order of the day, or rather night. At last a pause occurred, which enabled us to gather up the wounded; then, with a war-whoop and a ringing cheer, we rallied our broken forces for a "forlorn hope," and were about to sweep down on the defenders with the impetuosity of a mountain torrent, when lo! a mighty knocking was heard, and knowing well the hurricane of wrath it portended, the gallant warriors, like a lot of frightened hares, scampered off to the friendly shelter of their beds. As I had been in the hottest of the fray, and was the last to leave the scene of action, the steward with a full sweep bore down upon me. I was ordered to report myself at head-quarters next morning. Spanker—unlucky wight —was also seized. It was my first offending, but he was well known as the leader in every kind of mischief.

> He was what nurses call a "limb,"
> One of those misguided creatures
> Who, though their intellects are dim,
> Are one too many for their teachers.
> And if you asked of him to say
> What twice ten was, or three times seven,
> He'd glance (in quite a placid way)
> From heaven to earth, from earth to heaven.
> And not so much esteemed was he
> Of the authorities, and, therefore,
> He fraternised by chance with me,
> Needing a somebody to care for.
> And three fair summers did we twain
> Live (as they say) and love together,
> And bore by turns the wholesome cane,
> Till our young skins became as leather.

> And carved our names on every desk,
> And tore our clothes, and inked our hands,
> And looked unique and picturesque,
> And bore the cane upon our hands.
>   And seeing ignorance is bliss,
>   And wisdom consequently folly,
>   The obvious result is this—
>   That our two lives were very jolly.

When the steward had left the ward to its stillness, and Spanker and myself to our reflections, the other boys crowded round us, speculating on the extent and kind of our morning's punishment. It was the opinion of some of the more knowing that we should get off with "cakes" (which being translated into "town" lingo, means simply chastisement with a cane), whilst the more experienced of the older boys comforted us with the assurance that nothing short of a public "brushing" would satisfy the offended powers! Spanker had experienced both kinds of punishment, which he always received with a Spartan-like indifference, and he had the hardihood to assure me that the tickling sensation which permeated the system through a dose of the rod, *per flagellationem extremam,* was of the most agreeable description. For myself I had a righteous dread of the very word "flogging," but Spanker had conjugated that verb in all its tenses. We are told by Grose, and by the author of "Bacchus and Venus," that the word "flog" is a cant term. Be that as it may, it is in my opinion a word that ought not to be found in any school vocabulary, and I am happy to think that the "powers that be" of Christ's Hospital have come to the same conclusion, as it is now almost, though not entirely unknown within those classic walls. I am aware of the existence of a west-country proverb, which says that—

> A woman, a whelp, and a walnut tree,
> The more you bash them, the better they be.

My experience, however, of "bashing" is this—that the more boys are "bashed," the more hardened they become. Extreme corporal punishment deadens the moral faculties, and every "old Blue" will, I think, bear me out when I say that frequent punishment only made the boys more callous and indifferent, and turned into "bullies," boys whose nature had originally been companionable and kind.

Now, I had certainly nothing to hope for but the most condign punishment, for though I had not been the leader in the affair, I had had the misfortune to be caught, and so I was quite prepared to become the scapegoat of the rest. After breakfast the next morning the boys were all told to remain in their places, and in tones which could not be mistaken, the steward ordered the beadle to be sent for. I prepared myself for the worst, and I must have the candour to admit that the delightful sensations described by Spanker as resulting from the application of the prickly twig, were altogether beyond my powers of imagination.

"B——, my boy," said my co-partner in guilt, "we're in for it now. Don't blubber!"

When the beadle made his appearance, holding in his hand two of the most formidable instruments of torture I had ever seen, I began to think of Spanker's delightful theory, but failed to derive any satisfaction or comfort therefrom. When silence had been restored, and the steward had enlarged with much eloquence upon the enormity of our offence, Spanker was ordered to take down his clothes, which he did, in a manner which showed me that he had gone through a similar performance on many previous occasions. He was then ordered to "mount" the back of one of the menials, and the smile which broke over Spanker's features, as "stroke" succeeded "stroke," freely persuaded me that there was truth after all, in his boasted theory, as he seemed rather to like it than otherwise.

> O, ye gods and little fishes,
> What's a boy without his breeches?

I remember how Spanker looked without his, and I began to speculate what sort of a figure I should cut without mine! When the hardened young sinner had descended from the rack, the steward beckoned me to approach him, and I began involuntarily to "unbutton." Imagine my surprise to hear that he had made inquiries respecting my past conduct, and from what he could learn, he was convinced that I had not been an active promoter of the affair. He trusted that the punishment I had just witnessed would be a warning to me not to transgress any more, and concluded by ordering me to learn the 119th Psalm by heart, giving me two days to do it in, and the "laws, testimonies, statutes, commandments, judgments," and such like words which run through that interminable psalm, have been running in my head all through the battle of life.

The steward made impressions upon us occasionally, but only when we deserved it. Take him all in all, he was a kindly and considerate man, and his services to the Hospital entitle him to gratitude and respect. He is still in harness, although the able and energetic assistant steward, Mr. Wagner, relieves him of his most onerous duties.

When visiting the hospital on recent occasions, we were much struck with the warm bond of affection existing between Mr. Wagner and his little flock. Once inside the gates he was never alone, but always surrounded by a large army full of inquiries on subjects literary, political, and scientific. Mr. Wagner discards the cane, and governs by personal influence and example.

Life at Hertford.

The Hertford School is much better off than the larger one in Newgate Street in playground accommodation—possessing as it does an extensive field and "drill shed," where the boys are daily put through their facings by an experienced "drill master." They also have the advantage of charming country rambles; and what "Blue" does not remember the quaint old church and God's Acre, with the tall elm trees which have for centuries kept watch and ward over the peaceful sleepers in their long unbroken rest.

What a crowd of delightful memories does not "Morgan's Walk" conjure up, as after years of toil in "life's hard battle" we once more revisit the well-remembered scenes of childhood's happy days. In our strolls great care was exercised to prevent our coming in contact with the "Blues" of gentler mould (the girls). If we went to the right the lynx-eyed matron would immediately order them to file to the left; and I can safely say that during the whole of my time at Hertford no advancement was ever permitted *she*-wards, but we were strictly kept at that distance which is said "to lend enchantment to the view." Far be it from me to libel the softer sex in general, and the fair inmates of the school in particular, but I always had a shrewd suspicion that any little attention we were enabled stealthily to bestow when the vigilance of the matron was for a moment relaxed, was duly appreciated.

In my time the girls' school was not in a very thriving condition, and the number of inmates dwindled down considerably. Amongst the many changes which the Governors are contemplating, the entire remodelling of the girls' school is not the least interesting. It is proposed to add considerably to the number, and it is hoped they will see their way to alter the character of the dress, which has at the present time an unmistakable stamp of charity upon it, not only repugnant to the children but distasteful to their parents and the public.

"Every now and then," says a well-known author, writing of this time, "the monotony of our daily routine would be tragically, but not altogether unpleasingly, diversified by an execution. Some miserable urchin, whose round-hand would have run into a small-pox of blots, would be ordered into the dark lobby, between the inner and the outer door, at the far corner of the school. Four comrades, pressed into the hateful service, would accompany him; one would serve as horse, two of them would have a leg a-piece to hold secure, and the fourth would have the more ignoble task assigned him of holding tight over the wretch's head the extremity of his garments so as to leave exposed the orthodox surface for birch-correction. Meanwhile, over the listening schoolroom would be heard the sound as of a hailstorm, and stifled shrieks that seemed to issue from out a bull of Phalaris. Then the hailstorm would cease, and the shrieks would die away; and from the den would emerge the culprit, to be in the estimation of his school-fellows, a martyr for the day and a hero for a week.

I humbly but devoutly thank my stars that I was never so martyrized. It is not the physical pain that I would so strongly deprecate; for in my time I was often subjected to punishments more severe than the ordinary birch-flogging; and they left, for the most part, no permanent feeling of shame or anger behind them. The horror of the old time-honoured punishment consists in the unspeakably ludicrous position into which a poor fellow is hoisted between earth and heaven; a sight to set the gods on high Olympus roaring over their nectar with inextinguishable laughter. To this very day, and on this very day, they are guffawing at the tragico-comedy, as it is being enacted in the grammar schools of dear conservative, wilful, pig-headed old England."

Governors' Day is one of the red-letter days in the Hertford boys' calendar. It was the Hertford Carnival; and the best clue to its character and effect is given by the song with which it was ushered in :—" Or seree and or scrāa, a fellow going to pun on Governors' Day." Or seree I have since learnt was a corruption of all sereno; the or serāa was introduced like many another phrase in more aspiring poetry, *gratia metri*. It was kept as a general holiday, and the visiting Governors, who attend as a sort of deputation from the London Board, are deputed to inquire into the conduct of the boys, and the management of the school. It is an annual affair, and is no doubt looked upon by the worthy gentlemen as a capital day's "outing." In my time the rota happened to be a particularly jolly one, and high fun did we all have scrambling for apples, nuts, halfpence, &c., in the field. A dinner was always provided by the steward for his distinguished guests, to which the masters were invited, and there can be no doubt that the Governors usually returned to London very well pleased with all that they had witnessed.

"A very singular superstition," says D'Arcy Thompson, "was prevalent in this junior school in my time, and I have little doubt that it has descended by tradition. From a misinterpretation of a verse in the Athanasian Creed, it was supposed that the muttered repetition of the word 'Trinity' was a specific against all peril. Vicarious repetition was included in the doctrine. I have known a big fellow, when summoned unexpectedly to the master's desk, pass the order round for every one to say 'Trinity' for him as fast as possible; and for a few seconds there would be some fifty of us chattering the word as quickly as our tongues could move. Sometimes the charm failed; and vengeance would be taken by a bully upon the little wretches whom he logically supposed to have uttered the mystic word with insufficient vehemence, rapidity, and faith.

"There were also two terrible legends current, and universally believed. It was said that, many years ago, two infatuated boys had sinned beyond repentance in the following ways: one had said his prayers backwards; and the other had written a letter in his own blood to the Power of Evil, and placed it beneath his pillow before going to sleep. The morning after, the beds of both were found empty, and no tidings were ever heard of either.

"The cause and manner of their disappearance was horrible, but obvious. There were several big boys, whose statements admitted of no questioning, who had been told by the night-watchers that the ghosts of these miserable young sinners were continually seen after midnight in the infirmary back-yard.

"Underneath the writing-school were very extensive passages and cellars, forming a species of petty labyrinth. I ventured once a considerable way inside; but suddenly was seized with a panic, and scurried back to the light of day. This was the favourite haunt of an old man, named Bush, who was general scavenger and performer of all nasty work. He was probably the grimiest man in the world outside of Poland. Had the poet Æschylus once set eyes on him, he would have styled him in his own boldly figurative way, 'The Twin-brother of Dirt.'

"On all hands he was suspected, not without cause, of being an ogre. Bones in large quantities, were known to be stored up in his secret cave. One very big boy in my own sleeping-room once informed us that he had watched his time, when Bush was otherwise engaged, and had penetrated within the cave until he had reached a spot where was a kind of well, and round the well were great piles of bones. He had dipped his finger in the well, and to his horror had found that the liquid it contained was blood! The bones, therefore, were in all probability not beef or mutton bones! One little Paynim miscreant made some puerile suggestion about red-ink and dinner-remains; but he was at once summarily dealt with by the justly offended narrator, to the great satisfaction of all us believers, and to the entire removal of his own pestilent and unnatural incredulity.

"It was not long after the recital of these horrors that Bush left the service of the school, and he was frequently seen driving a gig upon the high road, with his face approximately clean and a white shirt on. The report current in the outer town was, that he had inherited a small fortune from a distant relative; but the people of the outer town knew nothing about the winding cellars, the pool of blood, and the huge heaps of human bones."

And now a word about the respected Head Master of our time — Rev. Nathaniel Keymer. All the masters had their own peculiar methods of punishment, and Mr. Keymer was rather partial to what we used to designate "tight breechings." When a youngster had offended him beyond forbearance, he would order him "over the form," and taking hold of his "unmentionables," would draw them tight, in order that the cane might find its way better to that part of the body where honour is generally supposed to rest. I shall never forget, on one occasion, when receiving a more than usually severe "tight breeching," I so rolled and roared that I upset the form on the worthy master's toes, and as I suspect he suffered somewhat from "corns," I was ordered to receive a second edition! On Sunday evenings, when the weather would not permit of our walk to church, we attended service in the dining-hall, on which occasions

Mr. Keymer officiated, and always commenced his sermon with the words "My dear children!" which was rather different from his Monday's exhortation, "Over the form!"

What Blue does not remember the fruitful garden, belonging to the Head Master, that adjoined the boys' field? I am afraid that the tempting fruit proved too much for many a watery mouth; and many were the daring expeditions improvised to obtain a closer inspection of the coveted apples and pears. I know well enough that we had a comforting theory that anything abstracted therefrom was only "taken," not "stolen." We have never heard whether Mr. Keymer held the same views—perhaps he was unable to realise the niceness of the distinction. Besides Mr. Keymer's garden, we were sorely tempted by the turnips of one Mullins, which were within easy access—only an easily surmounted wooden paling intervening. These turnips were apples of the Hesperides, watched incessantly by the dragons, Allen and Crossman. "At times," says an old Blue, "an adventurer would be gathering the sweet fruit into his lap for his comrades and himself, when Allen would drop as it were down from the clouds, and kindly assist the weeping trespasser to the right side of the frail boundary and march him off, with a numerous and sympathising, but mysteriously delighted escort, to the office of the superintendent, and the offender would be executed on the spot, untried and unshriven."

Needful reforms in the Hertford School now proceed at such a pace that Blues of the olden time would not recognise it. For nearly 300 years, the boys on the foundation were compelled to attend the service at church without a Bible. It was only in the year 1820, when one of the nurses, as a reward for good conduct, commenced making the boys a present of the sacred volume out of her own private funds, that the

Governors were ultimately shamed into supplying Bibles to the boys generally, but the name of Mrs. Moore, the nurse, ought to be held in affectionate remembrance for taking the initiative in such a good work.

There is a capital field at Hertford where the boys fly their kites, play at cricket, make tents, and go through drill. The diet is on a most liberal scale, and the discipline mild in the extreme. The boys have now a swimming-bath within easy access of the school, which is much patronised during the summer months. In fine weather the boys are taken by the beadle for a stroll through the surrounding country, which is noted for pleasant walks and hospitable homes. Occasionally the gentry of the neighbourhood drop in and get up a scramble amongst the boys.

During a recent visit to the Hertford School, before the sad suicide of the poor lad Gibbs, we had the pleasure of hearing from the Head Master, the Rev. J. H. Newnum, M.A., a most satisfactory account of the tone and discipline of the School, and were gratified beyond measure to hear that he was indebted, not to the cane or birch, the use of which he condemned, but to milder and more pleasurable influences. With Mr. Newnum as Head Master, Mr. Ludlow as Steward, and Mr. Wagner as assistant Steward, parents have a guarantee that their children will be properly—indeed affectionately—cared for.

CHAPTER VII.

SCHOOL LIFE IN LONDON.

T the age of eleven we "put away childish things," and became at once a man—in our own estimation—for had we not blossomed into a London swell? The School at Hertford was all very well for the small fry, but we would have none of it. We almost desired to forget that we had ever seen the place, not from ingratitude so much as self-importance, and it was a common habit with us, which is continued to this day, to call the little Hertford boys "cads." For four years we had been in the nursery with our toys; we were now in the world, or rather in a large, noisy city, wherein our individuality was merged in a great sea of life. We were brought into daily contact with boys, or rather young men, nearly twice our age, who used to "flop" their long hair in Grecian style, and "spadge" about to their own amusement and our admiration. But great as were the Grecians, there was another order which in our day took precedence—the boys of the Mathematical School. These desperadoes were the terror of the small boys, who would scamper away the moment the cry was raised, " The First-Order is coming ! " Writing of the Mathematical School Charles Lamb says, " Still these sea-boys answered some good purpose in the school. They were the military class amongst the boys—foremost in athletic exercises—and vindicators of its prowess far and near ; and the apprentices in the vicinage, and sometimes the butcher-boys in the neighbouring market, had sad occasions to test their valour."

The mode of admitting boys to the Mathematical

School was to say the least of it peculiar. Periodically a detachment of the "First-Order" would make a tour of the wards late at night, to take down the names of boys desirous of joining.

This ceremony was by no means a quiet one, as some may suppose. To take down the names of the boys was a small affair; the most important business consisted in making a tremendous row, and setting authority at defiance. The ward door on these occasions was closely watched by the monitor's boy, so that it might be opened directly the noisy shower of knocks set in, and then when the door was opened, half-a-dozen stentorian voices would shout at once "Who wants to be in the Royal Mathematical School?" The nurse looked on with fear and trembling, but spoke not. The monitors were obsequiously silent, and the Grecian kept his study. The mathematical night was looked to with much interest by the boys, who had no small admiration of these "King's boys," so named from the Royal Founder of the Mathematical School, Charles II. At the first drawing-room of the year, the boys are presented to the Sovereign, who graciously inspects their drawings.

During the illness of George III. these presentations were discontinued, but the Governors of the Hospital continued to pay £1 3s., the amount ordinarily received by each boy. The practice of receiving the children was revived by William IV.

Each of the "mathematical boys," having passed his Trinity House examination, and received testimonials of his good conduct, is presented with a watch worth from £9 to £13, in addition to an outfit of clothes, books, mathematical instruments, a Gunter's scale, a quadrant, and sea-chest.

During our stay in the London School from 1848-51, it was our privilege to occupy almost every official post—viz., Monitor's boy, Grecian's boy, Bell boy,

Bellows' boy, Jack boy, Platter boy, Lavatory boy, and above all, Beer boy, and ultimately the dignified position of monitor. All these appointments were considered prizes, and so were much sought after by the boys, as certain privileges were attached to each office. Our whole school life, at this present writing, is a pleasant memory. We forget the desolate moorlands and morasses here and there, and remember only the pleasant walks, and lasting friendships, and manly rivalries and healthy sports. There were, of course, occasional troubles to be got through, certain battles to be undertaken, and sundry chastisements—in most cases deserved—to be endured; but take it all in all, we were as happy as boys usually are away from home. Our games were perhaps a little rough, and the little fellows usually came in for the kicks and the big boys for the halfpence. "Beating the bear," "fly-the-garter," "gates," "prisoner's base," "French and English," "storming the castle," were perhaps the most popular amongst us. As a rule the different wards kept together in their amusements, except, as it occasionally happened, a trial of strength took place between them. In our time the boys were much given to "mivvies," or marbles, and some skilful fortunate youngsters would by the end of the marble season, amass an immense stock, and so become absolute merchants in them. "Fly-the-garter" was one of the unlawful games, and when played at it was requisite to keep watch for the lynx-eyed beadle, whose appearance would cause us to resume in "another degree." One game I well remember, and as I have not heard of it in any other school, I fancy it must be peculiarly a Christ's Hospital amusement. It was called "Good books," and was played by five boys in the following manner: five pieces of paper of exactly the same size and appearance are selected, and on each is written one or other of these words,

Rex, Judex, Opifex, Fur, and Castigator. The five pieces are then at a given signal thrown into the air, and each boy seizes one. The lucky holder of Rex (the king) calls forth Judex (the judge), to give instructions to Opifex (the watchman) to seize Fur (the thief), who is condemned by the judge to receive a number of strokes across the hand administered by Castigator.

The boys have now a field at Dulwich, where cricket and other sports are carried on every Wednesday and Saturday.

Giff's Cloister is the only relic left of the Greyfriars Monastery. It was known in our time as Giff's Cloister, from the fact that one of the beadles, George Isaac Fuller, kept watch and ward there.

He was an old man, and his "watch and ward" was not very strict, for all the rough and unlawful games were usually held under his very nose. In these rough games the small fry came off very badly, for if their little heads were not put into chancery, their tails were generally torn off, and youthful nectar was made to flow freely and fully. And no wonder, for the weapons used were formidable, consisting as they did, of leathern girdles with buckles attached, handkerchiefs twisted into knots, pieces of rope, and hardened practised fists, which had a nose attraction as powerful as the needle's to the pole.

In summer the boys repaired by detachments to Peerless Pool, attended by one or more of the beadles, who were armed with long poles to extend to bathers who by mischance got beyond their depth; and many were the attempts made by expert swimmers to drag the man of authority into the water—buttons and all.

This well known bath was formerly one of the springs that supplied the metropolis with water, when our ancestors drew that essential element from public conduits, that is to say, before the "old" waterworks at London Bridge, or the New River had been brought to London by Sir Hugh Myddelton.

The streams of this pool at that time were conveyed, for the convenience of the inhabitants near Lothbury, through pipes terminating "close to the south-west corner of the church."

Stow speaks of it as "a 'cleere' water called Perilous Pond."

What old Blue does not remember "Functious Alley," leading to the bath? And the "Half Circle," and "Nine's Corner," so named because one of nine was unfortunately drowned there, and "the Fan"— what pleasant memories they recall!

In connection with swimming, we must not omit mention of the fact that the Royal Humane Society's medal has recently been awarded to Archibald Douglas Maclean, a Blue, and that it was publicly presented to him, in December last, in the Great Hall of Christ's Hospital, Newgate Street, in the presence of the whole school. The circumstances under which the medal was awarded were as follows: On August 25, between five and six o'clock in the afternoon, Hereward Brackenbury, with some other children of Colonel Brackenbury, and young Maclean, a student of Christ's Hospital, were in a punt on the lake of the Royal Military College, Sandhurst. Hereward Brackenbury was leaning over the side of the boat, dragging a string with a piece of wood attached to it through the water, when his brother, who was rowing, 'caught a crab,' fell back, and knocking against him, pushed him into the water. Young Maclean was the first of the party to perceive the accident, the boy who caused it being prostrated on his back by the force of his false stroke, and immediately plunged in to the rescue with all his heavy clothing on, including his shoes, dived for him as he was sinking, and was immediately clutched by the neck, and had great difficulty in freeing himself and rising to the surface; but after a desperate struggle he succeeded in reaching the boat, and placing young Brackenbury safely on board. The danger incurred was very great, as the accident occurred in a depth of water from 12 feet to 15 feet, with a large quantity of thick weeds, between the two islands, not far from the spot where a few years since Major Taylor and his daughter were drowned.

The blue coat and yellow stockings still bear striking proof of the conservative feeling which reigns paramount in Christ's Hospital; whilst everything else in connection with the Hospital has undergone a change, the dress still remains a striking reminder of the monkish days.

Advocates of a more town-like costume ever and anon cast ridicule upon the yellow stockings, and the girdle, and the bands; and the small London boys make game at the dress, and country lads open wide their mouths at the sight of it; but after all everybody who knows anything about the school respects it; and in the City of London it is a sure passport to favour, and everywhere commands respect. "Our dress," says a well-known writer, "was of the coarsest and quaintest kind, but was respected out of doors, and is so. It consisted of a blue drugget gown, or body with ample skirts to it, a yellow vest underneath in winter time, small clothes of Russia duck, worsted yellow stockings, a leathern girdle, and a little black worsted cap, usually carried in the hand. I believe it was the ordinary dress of children in humble life during the reign of the Tudors. We used to flatter ourselves that it was taken from the monks, and there went a monstrous tradition that at one period it consisted of blue velvet with silver buttons. It was said, also, that during the blissful era of the blue velvet we had roast mutton for supper; but that the small clothes not being then in existence, and the mutton suppers too luxurious, the eatables were given up for the ineffables."

The yellow stockings in our day were on many occasions the cause of strife and sometimes bloodshed. One instance occurs to me.

It was a common remark with town boys that we had dipped our legs in the mustard-pot: that we had a yellow stomach and a blue skin, which the couplet went on to say were enough to make a certain individual (who shall be nameless) grin.

A boy of our time, who now occupies an important official position connected with elementary education in London, had been followed by a small army who kept up a tolerable shower of personal remark, with a chorus, again and again repeated, of "Charity, Charity, Charity!"

Now, Charity can stand a great deal—it suffereth long and is kind, and doth not behave itself unseemly, and charity, as we have been told, is a most excellent gift. It has been presented to us in every conceivable form by moralists and divines, and has been variously described and expounded; and whilst inculcated by precept it is too often dead before it can be exemplified by example.

But it was reserved to C—— to furnish this age with the most striking and telling example of the never-failing power of charity.

Turning to his tormentors, with charity ever on their lips, he selected the biggest representative, and with one drive, straight from the elbow, clave him to the ground, with this instructive reminder—Charity never faileth!

CHAPTER VIII.

SCHOOL PUNISHMENT.—FLOGGING.

THE barbarous modes of punishment that were at one time, unfortunately, common to all schools, and which seem to have been most unmercifully inflicted in our great public institutions, are now falling into disrepute; and, though not altogether abolished, are gradually being numbered with the things of the past. This is especially true of Christ's Hospital, where flogging is now seldom resorted to, and only for offences against morality, or for some grave infringement of the discipline of the school; but we have a painfully vivid recollection of a time not very remote when corporal chastisement was administered for offences which would now escape with a much lighter punishment. This system of terrorism was bad for all concerned; it tended to brutalise the masters, to make the strong, hardy boy callous, and the impatient, irritable boy reckless; but those who suffered most intensely were the meek, the sensitive, and the shy—to whom school life was often, through the harshness of the masters, a positive torture. Indeed, it is not too much to say that many a boy of fair capacity has, from sheer fright, been rendered a hopelessly incorrigible dunce; and the power of tradition, the influence of custom, could hardly be better illustrated than by the fact that, for generation after generation, and century after century, successive masters followed the old bad system, and never seem to have reflected that birching a boy to make him learn was, to say the least of it, working at the wrong end. In these days, happily, humanity and common sense are getting the upper

hand, so that in our remarks about flogging we refer, in speaking of Christ's Hospital, to a state of things that has passed away.

Charles Lamb gives the following account of the effect produced on his mind by the school punishments in vogue in his day, some of which, antiquated and barbarous enough in all conscience, he describes:—
"I was a hypochondriac lad," he says, " and the sight of a boy in fetters upon the day of my first putting on the blue clothes, was not exactly fitted to assuage the natural terrors of initiation. I was of tender years, barely turned of seven, and had only read of such things in books, or seen them but in dreams. I was told he had *run away*. This was the punishment for the first offence. As a novice, I was soon after taken to see the dungeons. These were little square Bedlam cells, where a boy could just lie at his length upon straw and a blanket—a mattress, I think, was afterwards substituted—with a peep of light, let in askance, from a prison orifice at top, barely enough to read by. Here the poor boy was locked in by himself all day, without sight of any but the porter, who brought him his bread and water, *who might not speak to him*, or of the beadle, who came twice a week to call him out to receive his periodical chastisement.

"The culprit who had been a third time an offender, and whose expulsion was at this time deemed irreversible, was brought forth, as at some solemn *auto da fé*, arrayed in uncouth and most appalling attire, and all trace of his late 'watchet weeds' being carefully effaced, he was exposed in a jacket resembling those which London lamplighters formerly delighted in, with a cap of the same. The effect of this divestiture was such as the ingenious devisers of it must have anticipated. With his pale and frightened features, it was as if some of those disfigurements in Dante had seized upon him. In this disguisement he was brought into the hall, where awaited him the whole number of his schoolfellows, whose joint lessons and sports he was henceforth to share no more; the awful presence of the steward, to be seen for the last time; of the executioner-beadle, clad in his state robe for the occasion; and of two faces more, of direr import, because never but in these extremities visible. These were Governors, two of whom, by choice of charter, were always accustomed to officiate at these *ultima supplicia*—not to mitigate (so, at least, we understood it), but to enforce the uttermost stripe. Old Bamber Gascoigne and Peter Aubert, I remember, were colleagues on one occasion, when the beadle turning rather pale, a glass of brandy was ordered to prepare him for the mysteries. The scourging was, after the old Roman fashion, long and stately. The lictor accompanied the criminal quite round the hall. We were generally too faint with attending to the previous disgusting circumstances to make accurate report with our eyes of the degree of corporal suffering inflicted. After scourging, he was made over in his *san benito* to his friends, if he had any, or to his parish officer, who, to enhance the effect of the scene, had his station allotted to him on the outside of the hall gate."

"'The discipline at Christ's Hospital, in my time,' says Coleridge, in his "Table-Talk," "was ultra-Spartan; all domestic ties were to be put aside. 'Boy!' I remember Boyer saying to me once, when I was crying, the first day of my return after the holidays, 'boy! the school is your father; boy! the school is your mother; boy! the school is your brother; the school is your sister; the school is your first cousin, and your second cousin, and all the rest of your relations. Let's have no more crying!' No tongue can express good Mrs. Boyer. Val Le Grice and I were once going to be flogged for some domestic misdeed, and Boyer was thundering away at us by way of prologue, when Mrs. B. looked in, and said, 'Flog them soundly, sir, I beg!' This saved us. Boyer was so nettled at the interruption, that he growled out, 'Away! woman, away!' and we were let off."

Of this same Dr. Boyer, for many years headmaster of the School, some very curious anecdotes are told, the scenes described being amusing enough to read of now, though they must have been anything but pleasant for some of those who took part in them.

"Nothing was more common," says Charles Lamb, "than to see him make a headlong entry into the school-room from his inner recess or library, and with turbulent eye, singling out a lad, roar out, 'Od's my life, sirrah' (his favourite adjuration), 'I have a great mind to whip you,' then with as sudden a retracting impulse, fling back into his lair, and after a cooling lapse of some minutes (during which all but the culprit had totally forgotten the context) drive headlong out again, piecing out his imperfect sense, as if it had been some devil's litany, with the expletory yell, 'And I will too.' In his gentler moods, when the *rabidus furor* was assuaged, he had resort to an ingenious method, peculiar, from what I have heard, to himself, of whipping the boy and reading the debates at the same time; a paragraph and a lash between, which in those times, when parliamentary oratory was most at a height and flourishing in these realms, was not calculated to impress the patient with a veneration for the diffuser graces of rhetoric.

"Once, and but once, the uplifted rod was known to fall ineffectual from his hand, when droll, squinting W. having been caught putting the inside of the master's desk to a use for which the architect had clearly not designed it, to justify himself with great simplicity averred, 'that he did not know the thing had been forewarned.'

"This exquisite irrecognition of any law antecedent to the oral or declaratory, struck so irresistibly upon the fancy of all who heard it (the pedagogue himself not excepted) that remission was unavoidable."

"When you were out in your lesson," says Leigh Hunt, speaking of the same worthy, "he turned upon you a round staring eye like a fish; and he had a trick of pinching you under the chin, and by the lobes of the ears, till he would make the blood come.

"He has many times lifted a boy off the ground in this way.

"He was indeed a proper tyrant, passionate and capricious, would take violent likes and dislikes, fondle some without any apparent reason, though he had a leaning to the servile, and perhaps to the sons of rich people: and he would persecute others in a manner truly frightful."

Leigh Hunt tells an amusing anecdote of the rendering of a dialogue between a missionary and an Indian—a reading which one of the boys, through an utter disregard of punctuation, rendered in a manner altogether original.

Boyer had received special instructions 'to look after the boy,' which duty he thoroughly carried out. The boy who was to be looked after usually took his place within reach of Boyer's fist, in order the better to receive his polite attentions.

The dialogue opens with a severe admonition from the master:

MASTER.—"Now, young man, have a care, or I'll set you a swinging task" (a common phrase of his).

PUPIL (not remembering his stop at the word missionary).—"Missionary can you see the wind?"

(Boyer gives him a slap on the cheek.)

PUPIL (raising his voice to a cry).—" Indian no!"

BOYER.—" God's—my—life young man! have a care how you provoke me!"

PUPIL (always forgetting the stop).—" Missionary how do you know there is such a thing?"

(Here a terrible thump.)

PUPIL (with a shout of agony).—" Indian because I feel it."

Here is one more anecdote of the master's cruelty:—" Amongst the boys that he 'spited' was one C., and every opportunity of punishing the object of his dislike was eagerly seized.

"On one occasion, the master in coming into the school saw C. in the middle of it with three other boys. He was not in one of his worst humours, and did not seem inclined to punish them till he saw C——.

"He then turned to one of the Grecians and said, 'I have not time to flog all these boys; make them draw lots, and I'll punish one.'

"The lots were drawn, and C—— was favourable. 'Oh, oh!' returned the master when he saw them, 'you have escaped, have you, sir?' and pulling out his watch, and turning again to the Grecian, observed that he found he *had* time to punish the whole lot, 'and, sir,' added he to C——, with another slap, 'I'll begin with you.'"

One of the boys when receiving punishment from Boyer, was in the habit of twisting himself about the master's legs, exclaiming at every stroke, "Oh, good God! consider my father, sir; my father, sir; you know my father!" whilst another boy, P——, afterwards a popular preacher, would snatch his jokes out of the very flame and fury of the master, like snapdragon. When receiving chastisement, he would dance round his executioner like a performing bear, and clapping his hand on that part of his body which received the stroke, would exclaim each time, "Oh, Lord!" making faces to the other boys the while.

It is told of Coleridge that when he heard of his old master's death, he remarked that it was lucky that the cherubim who took him to Heaven were nothing but faces and wings, or he would infallibly have flogged them by the way.

It is only fair to Dr. Boyer, however, to remember that at the time in which he flourished, all punishments were barbarous, and that many wretched criminals were hanged almost every week for offences which we should now consider amply expiated by a few days' imprisonment.

A writer in the *Chelmsford Chronicle*, an old "Blue," speaking of the School in 1798, says:—

"Now, on the topic of flogging, I can't resist relating a plan the master adopted to put a stop to fighting, which was of frequent occurrence, as the black eyes and broken noses would tell. When he saw a boy with marks on his face, he would call him out, and insist on his telling who his opponent was; if he was a fellow-grammarian he was called out; if he was in the writing school, Franklin would send for him (with his compliments to the writing-master); he would order out two brooms, select from them the best and longest twigs, and with them make two rods; he then made both boys strip their backs, and having planted them on the large table, gave each one a rod, and insisted on their flogging each other, promising that he who first gave in, should be then flogged in some other quarter. At it the boys would go, first very softly, but as they warmed, it was no joke; at last one gave in; down he was had, and it was "Unstrip, sir,"—"horse him, monitors," and the master used up the remnant of the rods on him. The nurses were permitted to flog and punish the boys as they thought proper, and some of the nurses were cruel old hags. One poor fellow in my ward was labouring under a bodily infirmity. The brute of a nurse used constantly to flog him with nettles, fresh gathered from time to time, for the purpose, declaring they had the virtue of strengthening his bodily frame."

"My father," adds this writer, "and the grammar-master were very intimate to my cost, for I used to be flogged or caned more frequently than other boys,—'out of regard to your father, sir,' he'd say, 'to get you on.' Alas! I was always so frightened when I went up to say my lessons, lest I should not say them correctly, that though I had them perfectly by heart while in my seat, my memory would fail me the instant the dreadful words, 'Now, sir, go on,' sounded in my ear, till at length I turned out a regular dunce."

A remarkable flogging oration delivered by a master of our own day deserves to be recorded.

W—— detected a boy in the very act of "fudging"—a crime of the deepest dye.

The culprit was forthwith ordered out for immediate execution. The windows were closed, the beadle sent for, and the whole class ordered to stand up to witness the performance. After lecturing the boy for about ten minutes on the enormity of his offence, W—— concluded with the following memorable peroration:—

"Boy, you have deceived your father! you have deceived your mother! you have deceived your governor! you have deceived your master! you have deceived yourself! you have deceived your God! —take down your breeches!"

But, after all, as the accompanying illustration will show, if the students of Christ's Hospital were chastised with whips, those of the public schools to which the sons of "the upper ten thousand" are sent, are tormented by scorpions. The difference in weight between the Eton birch of 12 ounces and the Christ's Hospital birch of 3½ ounces is very considerable; the difference in leverage—which in this case means, after all, the power of hard hitting—is something enormous. A modern "Blue" may rejoice that, having happily escaped the misfortune of being the son of a Peer, he is not black and blue; and if the sinning scholars in another institution, not removed by very many miles from Eton, are birched with equal, or more, severity, their condition at times must be quite "Harrowing."

Anecdotes of the birch in other schools are somewhat out of place here, but we cannot resist quoting the following :—

When a boy called on Dr. Keate, of Eton, to take leave, the worthy man remarked, "You seem to know me very well, but I have no recollection of ever having seen your face before."—"You are better acquainted with my other end," was the unblushing reply.

A similar anecdote has been versified as follows :—

An old Etonian once met Keate abroad
And seized his hand ; but he was rather floored
To see the Doctor seemed to know him not ;
"Doctor," quoth he, "you've flogged me oft, I wot ;
And yet it seems that me you've quite forgot."
"E'en now," says Keate, "I cannot guess your name,
The backs of boys are very much the same."

The famous Dr. Busby, of Westminster, was a notorious wielder of the birch, and before flogging a boy on one occasion, he is said to have published the banns as follows :—

"I publish the banns of matrimony between this rod and this boy; if any of you know just cause or impediment why they should not be united, you are to declare it."

The boy himself called out, "I forbid the banns."

"For what cause?" enquired the Doctor. "Because," said the boy, "the parties are not agreed."

The doctor allowed the validity of the objection, and the boy escaped.

CHAPTER IX.

THE SCHOOL FOOD.

IN few things, probably, was the wisdom of our ancestors less conspicuous than in those matters relating to the laws of Health. Of the simplest sanitary regulations they seem to have had no conception, nor did they understand the great importance of proper diet, especially for growing lads. Indeed, to judge by their practice, it must have been an axiom with the heads of our educational institutions that only hard fare, and little of it, was needed to make a hardy boy. Vitality is strong in childhood, and it says something for the latent power and vigour of the English race that (comparatively) so little mischief was done by the mode in which the boys of Christ's Hospital were fed for generations. Improvements have been gradually introduced, and now there is certainly no ground for complaint on that score; but if we look back even thirty or forty years we shall be surprised to see with what singular tenacity some bad old customs still lingered. It was not that the ruling powers were careless or intentionally unkind, but that they followed the traditions of the past somewhat too blindly, and, as Hood truly says,

"Evil is wrought by want of thought,
As well as want of heart."

In these days the Blue-Coat boys, happier in this respect than their predecessors, are well and abundantly fed, but matters were very different two hundred, one hundred, or even fifty years ago, and in fact the radical change for the better now observable, is quite a modern innovation, and one of which old "Blues," not yet of middle age, would have been only too glad in their time. There are stories, as we shall presently see, to the effect that in olden times the boys did not get even the scanty allowance apportioned to them by the rules, but, though here as elsewhere there may have been instances of occasional misconduct on the part of minor officials in this respect, there is no sufficient evidence of anything like systematic fraud, and, indeed, the short commons of the boys were generally far too short to allow of any material abbreviation.

We find some particulars of the Blue-Coat School and of the mode in which the scholars lived, in the "Antiquities of London," published in 1740, from which we should judge that workhouse boys in the present day would look with contempt on the diet of the "Blues" a century and a half ago. "Their manner of fare," says the author, speaking of the scholars of Christ's Hospital at that day, "is as follows:—They have every morning for their breakfast, bread and beer. On Sundays, they have boiled beef and the pottage for their dinners, and legs and shoulders of mutton for their suppers. On Tuesdays and Thursdays the same dinners as on Sundays. On the other days no flesh meat; on Mondays milk pottage, on Wednesdays furmity, on Fridays old pease and pottage, on Saturdays water gruel. They have roast beef twelve days in the year. Their supper is bread and cheese, or butter. Only on Wednesdays and Fridays they have pudding pies."

Nearly sixty years later, in 1798, according to a recent writer, matters were not much better. "In my ward," he says, "there stood every morning in the lower room one large tub (like a cooling tub in a brewhouse) filled with water; all the ward washed in this, a bowl of soft soap standing by it, and wiped themselves on one large jack-towel that hung behind the door, and was changed only once a week. The breakfast bell rang about seven, when we all went into the hall, the nurses following, with boys from each ward (called "bread-boys") carrying large baskets on their shoulders containing bread, which were taken to the head of each table, where stood the nurse, who, after "grace," went down the table, serving out to each boy half of a two-penny loaf of bread. 'Well,' you'll say, 'but where's the butter?' None was allowed—nothing but bare bread... Those who had been sparing overnight to save a portion of the small piece of cheese they had for their supper, pulled it out of their pockets. Sometimes a great fellow would make a little boy always supply him with cheese of mornings, out of the piece the poor fellow had had for his supper the night previous. Beer we had certainly, served out in wooden vessels of an extraordinary shape, called 'piggins'; about six of them for four boys to drink out of, but such beer! The piggins were seldom replenished, for we could not drink it. We used to call it 'the washings of the brewer's aprons.'"

Leigh Hunt, writing on the same subject, says:— "To say the truth, we were not too well fed at that time, either in quantity or quality; and we could not enter with our hungry imaginations into these remote philosophies. Our breakfast was bread and water, for the beer was too bad to drink. The bread consisted of the half of a three-halfpenny loaf, according to the prices then current. This was not much for growing boys, who had had nothing to eat from six or seven o'clock the preceding evening. For dinner we had the same quantity of bread, with meat only every other day, and that consisting of a small slice, such as you would give to an infant three or four years old. Yet even that, with all our hunger, we very often left half eaten—the meat was so tough. On the other days we had a milk-porridge, ludicrously thin; or rice-milk, which was better. There were no vegetables or puddings. Once a month we had roast beef, and twice a year (I blush to think of the eagerness with which it was looked for) a dinner of pork. One was roast and the other boiled; and on the latter occasion we had our only pudding, which was of peas. I blush to remember this; not on account of our poverty, but on account of the sordidness of the custom. There had much better been none. For supper we had a like piece of bread, with butter or cheese; and then to bed, with what appetite we might."

Nor does Charles Lamb, who was an inmate of the school some few years previously, speak more favourably of the diet. He says:—"I remember L—— at school, and can well recollect that he had some peculiar advantages which I and others of his school-fellows had not. His friends lived in town, and were near at hand; and he had the privilege of going to see them, almost as often as he wished, through some invidious distinction, which was denied to us. The present worthy sub-treasurer to the Inner Temple can explain how that happened. He had his tea and hot rolls in a morning, while we were battening upon our quarter of a penny loaf—our 'crug'—moistened with attenuated small beer, in wooden piggins, smacking of the pitched leathern jack it was poured from. Our Monday's milk porridge, blue and tasteless, and the pease-soup of Saturday, coarse and choking, were enriched for him with a slice of 'extraordinary bread and butter' from the hot loaf of the Temple. The Wednesday's mess of millet, somewhat less repugnant

—(we had three banyan to four meat days in the week)—was endeared to his palate by a lump of double-refined, and a smack of ginger (to make it go down the more glibly), or the fragrant cinnamon. In lieu of our *half-pickled* Sundays, or quite fresh boiled beef on Thursdays (strong as *caro equina*), with detestable marigolds floating in the pail, to poison the broth—our scanty mutton scrags on Fridays, and rather more savoury but grudging portions of the same flesh, rotten, roasted, or rare, on the Tuesdays (the only dish which excited our appetites and disappointed our stomachs in almost equal proportion)—he had his hot plate of roast veal, or the more tempting griskin (exotics unknown to our palates), cooked in the paternal kitchen (a great thing), and brought him daily by his maid or aunt. I remember the good old relative (in whom love forbade pride), squatted down upon some odd stone in a by-nook of the cloisters, disclosing the viands (of higher regale than those cates which the ravens administered to the Tishbite), and the contending passions of L—— at the unfolding. There was love for the bringer; shame for the thing brought and the manner of its bringing; sympathy for those who were too many to share in it, and, at top of all, hunger (oldest, strongest of the passions!) predominant, breaking down the strong fences of shame and awkwardness, and a troubling over-consciousness. . . .

"Under the stewardship of Perry, can L—— have forgotten the cool impunity with which the nurses used to carry away openly, in open platters, for their own tables, one out of two of every hot joint which the careful matron had been seeing scrupulously weighed out for our dinners?"

Things have altered very much since Lamb's time, and even since the time of the grandchildren of Lamb's contemporaries. From the experiences of a

"Blue" written in 1821, we learn that the boys of that day had nothing beyond a piece of bread for breakfast, and the writer waxes warm and eloquent over the wish that certain people had expressed, that butter should be added thereto. He considers that the addition of butter would make the boys effeminate and teach them expensive and luxurious habits (!) A few years after the date given above, however, a terrible innovation was introduced into the school. Milk and water—or, rather, water and milk—for the watery element largely preponderated, was introduced at the morning meal, and "sky-blue" has retained its place ever since. The writer quoted above also gives us the following weekly dietary. Sunday, roast beef; Monday, milk porridge; Tuesday, roast mutton; Wednesday, rice milk with bread and butter; Thursday, another dose of roast mutton; Friday, boiled mutton; Saturday, pea soup with bread and butter. The boys ate their meat off flat wooden trenchers, about nine inches square, as gravy was unknown in those days. The soup was served up in wooden bowls, and each boy was furnished with a wooden spoon. The beer was taken into the dining-hall in leathern jacks, and then poured into wooden piggins.

Our friend, therefore, could hardly charge the authorities with a desire to make the boys in any way effeminate. What would he say to the "powers that be" of the present day?

The dietary scale, as now framed, is liberal in the extreme. The general breakfast for each boy consists of $7\frac{1}{2}$ oz. of bread, and half-a-pint of milk, with or without hot or cold water, as the boys please; the special breakfast (in cases where it is ordered by the medical officer) comprises, in addition to the above-named allowance of bread, half-an-ounce of butter and 4 oz. of cold meat, with cocoa or coffee. The Grecians have $7\frac{1}{2}$ oz. of bread, 1 oz. of butter, and

8 oz. of cold meat, or 4 oz. of bacon, and a pint of coffee; the Monitors 7½ oz. of bread, 1 oz. of butter, and a pint of coffee.

The general dinner consists each day of 3 oz. of bread, and, on Monday, 4 oz. of mutton, and 8 oz. of potatoes; on Tuesdays, 4 oz. of pork, 4 oz. of potatoes, and an allowance of greens; on Wednesdays, 4 oz. of mutton and 8 oz. of potatoes; on Thursdays, 4 oz. of beef and 8 oz. of potatoes; on Fridays 4 oz. of mutton, 4 oz. of potatoes, and an allowance of greens; on Saturdays 4 oz. of beef and 8 oz. of potatoes; on Sundays 4 oz. of beef or veal, and 8 oz. of potatoes. Half-a-pint of ale is allowed to each boy on Mondays, Wednesdays and Fridays, and on two days in the week each boy has 6 oz. of Yorkshire pudding in addition to the rest of the ration, while occasionally 4 oz. of suet pudding are also allowed.

It should be added, moreover, that some little variety is introduced into the customary bill of fare, so that the boys have, about once in three weeks, hash, and about once in four weeks, meat pies instead of joints; once a fortnight, or thereabouts, moreover, they luxuriate in stewed rabbits. In hot weather beef is substituted for pork on the Tuesdays. About eighty boys, it should be remarked, have half-a-pint of ale daily, instead of three days a week only.

The Grecians' dinner is the same as that of the rest of the boys, only that they have a double allowance of meat, 1 oz. of cheese, and a pint of ale daily. The only difference in favour of the monitors, as compared with the scholars generally, is that they have half a pint of ale every day.

The general supper consists of 6 oz. of bread, ¾ of an ounce of butter, and a half pint of milk and water. The late supper for some two hundred of the elder boys is 4 oz. of bread and 1 oz. of cheese. Any boy asking for it may have an extra supply of bread at any meal, for which purpose an additional quantity is always sent up; while the supply of animal food is so far in excess of the requirements of the scholars that some 200 lbs. of meat and dripping are given away in fragments to the poor every week.

The writer above noticed, who objected to the luxury of butter with the bread of the boys, will be still further distressed—supposing him still to survive —to learn that not only are the scholars initiated into the expensive and effeminate habits indicated in the foregoing dietary scale, but that they now luxuriate in clean and wholesome earthenware, instead of eating from wooden trenchers and bowls.

The Hertford diet in 1866 was not, apparently, so good as at the present day, but it at least displayed a marked improvement on that furnished during the first half of the century. "For breakfast," says a "Blue" who was at Hertford in the year we have mentioned, "we had a hunk of bread and a bowl of lukewarm milk; and the same for tea, with the addition of an allowance of butter. It might be thought that such fare, however excellent, would become after a very long time, slightly distasteful. But this, owing to the ingenuity of the fellows in devising ways of dressing it, was not the case. I can only mention two or three. Perhaps the most usual method was to crumble up the bread fine into the milk, and then to stir the mixture till it became a thin curd. But others preferred to make a much thicker compost, more of the consistency of dough; this I have known us sometimes carry away by stealth and bake in the ward kitchen. But the more refined of us used to put our parts in whole, crusts and all, and then peck at them genteelly with our spoons, like birds. But now it is quite different; and on reliable authority I can announce to the world at large that the fellows are now used, actually used, to porridge, cocoa, and treacle. For dinner we had usually beef and mutton, but sometimes pork. As one or two joints did for forty of us, of course we could not expect gravy; but what we got instead of it was an excellent substitute. On Saturday, however, we had a treat. This was our soup day. It would be impossible to enumerate the dainties which went to the making up of this quasi-beverage. Certainly mangel-wurzels and turnip-tops were amongst the ingredients; and report darkly whispered that potato-parings and the leavings of the week were not wholly absent."

Whatever the suspicious ingredients of the soup of 1866 may have been, we can hardly doubt that it was a very much more nutritious and appetising article of food than the water-gruel served out to hungry little "Blues" on the Saturdays of a hundred years ago.

Here, again, is another contrast to the dietary of the last century, as to which we have the evidence of a perfectly independent witness—the *New York Herald*, of 1871 :—" Taking their seats, the lads below gave themselves up to jabbering, what time divers of the smaller boys passed to them their dinner, consisting of beef, Yorkshire pudding, potatoes, bread, and beer. There was no dessert of any kind, but the provisions looked good and appetising, and were plentifully supplied, most of the youths, not having before their eyes the fear of the fate of Oliver Twist, sending their plates a second or even a third time to the matrons who presided in state at the head of each table."

That the boys in the days before a reform of the dietary was instituted had no relish for their hard fare is plain enough from the old school rhyme—proof positive that the then youngsters, who must be anything but youngsters now, could not altogether appreciate the toughening process. Thus, as all Crugs will well remember, runs the verse :—

> "Sunday, all saints;
> Monday, all souls;
> Tuesday, all trenchers;
> Wednesday, all bowls;
> Thursday, tough Jack;
> Friday, no better;
> Saturday, pea-soup with bread and butter."

To sum up the whole of this portion of the matter, times have changed, and manners with the times. When the present dining-room is razed to the ground it will be able to tell a very different tale from its predecessor in use for a hundred and forty years, and which was redolent of "swipes" and "hard crug."

In giving the boys meat on every day of the week the authorities have wisely turned to account some of the strange and unique bequests made to the Hospital —bequests to which we have referred in another chapter.

CHAPTER X.

GRECIANS AND MONITORS.

IT may seem—indeed, we may as well at once admit that it is—trite and commonplace to say that no human institution is perfect, and that power, in whatever hands it may be placed, is sometimes liable to abuse; but, judging from much that has been written lately, it does appear necessary that the world should be reminded of these time-honoured axioms, as well as of the equally well known truth that the occasional abuse is no argument against the use of authority. If

> "Man, vain man,
> Dressed in a little brief authority,
> Plays such fantastic tricks before high heaven
> As make the angels weep,"

it is very proper that he should be punished for his

cruelty and arrogance; but to say that no man should have any authority in future because one occasionally makes bad use of it, would be to destroy all those bonds by which society is held together. And what is true of men is equally true of boys. Every one who knows anything of a large public school is, or should be, well aware that without something like the monitorial system the discipline of the school could scarcely be maintained with any degree of efficiency. And we venture to say that, though the monitors may sometimes use their power tyrannically, on the whole the system works well, and often protects the small and weakly boy from oppression on the part of his superiors in size and strength. Even on occasions when the monitor abuses his power, he is often tempted to do so by the feeling which prevails amongst schoolboys generally, and is particularly strong in the case of public schoolboys, that there is something dishonourable, mean, and cowardly in complaining to the superior of the harshness of the inferior authorities—a feeling which, though it may sometimes be carried to an absurd excess, is in the main wholesome and healthy. Of course particular care should be taken in the selection of boys to act as monitors, while the higher powers should exercise due vigilance in seeing that the monitorial office is not abused, or made the instrument for exercising a petty but provoking tyranny. We speak from personal experience when we say that for our own part we found it quite possible for a monitor in 1851 to maintain the discipline of the school without knocking the boys about, and, moreover, without finding it necessary to report a single boy to the Steward. A monitor who chooses to break the rules of the institution by inflicting corporal punishment on his own account, no doubt deserves degradation from his office and to undergo such further penalty as the gravity of the offence would seem to require; but it is preposterous to argue that because a monitor may now and then be cruel, monitors as a body should be "improved from off the face of the earth."

But, before we consider the position, privileges, and responsibilities of monitors, we must refer to that still higher order of beings, the Grecians, to whom some passing allusion was made in the chapter on "Famous Blues." The Grecians are now a far more numerous body than in the olden days, when very often only one or two were admitted to the dignity in the course of the year; but now, as then, their position in the school is such that they are looked up to with an amount of reverence, approaching, indeed, to absolute awe, which to an outsider is simply incomprehensible. "When I entered the school," says Leigh Hunt, "I was shown three gigantic boys—young men, rather (for the eldest was between seventeen and eighteen) —who, I was told, were going to the University. These were the Grecians. They were the three head boys of the grammar-school, and were understood to have their destiny fixed for the Church. The next class to these—like a college of cardinals to those three popes (for every Grecian was in our eyes infallible)—were the deputy-Grecians. The former were supposed to have completed their Greek studies, and were deep in Sophocles and Euripides. The latter were thought equally competent to tell you anything respecting Homer and Demosthenes."

On St. Matthew's Day (Sept. 21) the Grecians delivered orations before the Lord Mayor, corporation, governors, and their friends, a relic of the scholars' disputations in the cloisters. Christ's Hospital by ancient custom possesses the privilege of addressing the sovereign, on the occasion of his or her coming into the City, to partake of the hospitality of the corporation of London. On the visit of Queen Victoria in 1837 a booth was erected for the Hospital boys in St. Paul's Churchyard, and on the royal carriage reaching the cathedral west gate the senior scholar, with the head master and treasurer, advanced to the coach-door and delivered a congratulatory address to her Majesty, with a copy of the same on vellum.

Mr. Howard Staunton, writing in 1869, says :— " On an average four scholars are annually sent to Cambridge with an Exhibition of £80 a year, tenable for four years, and one to Oxford with £100 a year for the like period. Besides these there are the 'Pitt Club' Scholarship and the 'Times' Scholarship, each of £30 a year for four years, which are awarded by competition to the best scholar in classics and mathematics combined, and held by him in addition to his general Exhibition. Upon proceeding to the University each Grecian receives an allowance of £20 for books, £10 for apparel, and £30 for caution-money and settling-fees."

The dress of the Grecians is superior to that of the other boys, they have a study to themselves, and various little luxuries denied to others; they have also the very enviable privilege of visiting their friends at any time out of school hours; they are not considered to require surveillance.

It requires a rare combination of ability and perseverance to arrive at the class from which the Grecians are selected. When it is considered that a boy has to work his way through five classes with an undermaster before he is eligible for "the little Erasmus," the lowest class of the upper school, it will be understood that he has to go through a great deal of labour to reach this point—so much so that many boys leave the school at fifteen years of age without having gained even this promotion. But, presuming that the scholar is advanced thus far, it is necessary that he should raise himself another step and become a " great Erasmus " boy. If he should acquire this position he may be selected, after an examination in classics, as a deputy-Grecian, and should he distinguish himself in that capacity he will at last attain the highest point of his ambition—so far as the school is concerned—and rejoice in the full-blown honours of a Grecian. A boy arrives at this dignity at the age of fifteen, and continues on the foundation till he is twenty, when he proceeds either to Oxford or Cambridge University. Probationers are now appointed, who compete for the Grecian's position.

"These youths," says Charles Lamb, writing of the Grecians of his period, "from their superior acquirements, their superior age and stature, and the fewness of their numbers (for seldom above two or three at a time were inaugurated into that high order), drew the eyes of all, and especially of the younger boys, into a reverent observance and admiration. How tall they used to seem to us! how stately would they pace along the cloisters! while the play of the lesser boys was absolutely suspended, or its boisterousness at least allayed, at their presence! Not that they ever beat or struck the boys. That would have been to have demeaned themselves—the dignity of their persons alone insured them all respect. The task of blows, of corporal chastisement, they left to the common monitors, or heads of wards."

As will be inferred from some of the foregoing remarks, the monitor and marker is a very important person in the economy of each ward. The boys chosen to fill this office must have gained a certain *locus standi* in the grammar school, and have attracted the attention of the Steward for their good behaviour. This species of promotion by merit alone exercises a very happy effect, inasmuch as it opens a field of advancement to every boy. According to your attainments in the classics when you enter the school, so is your place in the ward, as also at the dinner table. In proportion as you make progress in your studies, and as new boys are received, so you advance step by step to the top of the table; and when you have arrived there, provided your conduct has been uniformly correct, the steward appoints you to be a monitor. It rests with the head grammar-master to name you a marker, but it rarely happens that he offers any objection to the recommendation of the steward, although such instances do occasionally take place. Immediately you are appointed monitor and marker, and have received "the seals of office," in the shape of a silver medal, which you are expected to wear on Sundays, suspended by a blue ribbon to the button-hole, your newly-acquired dignity forbids your association with any but your equals. It is considered an act of condescension on your part to join in any of the games after your instalment. "It was with no small amount of pride," writes a fellow monitor, "that I left the steward's office after my promotion; and the first time I paraded up and down the table, whilst the boys were dining, my attention was absorbed in an endeavour to discover whether the boys were awed by my dignified bearing, or amused at my embarrassed deportment. Monitors have a very arduous, and sometimes unpleasant office, for they were, and I believe are, held accountable for all the misdemeanours committed in their wards. On the other hand, they had many privileges to counterbalance what was disagreeable. An extra quantity of rations, a cupboard to yourself, and a boy to wait upon you, are no mean comforts in the eyes of a schoolboy. Moreover, they might sit up until ten o'clock, whilst the boys generally retired to bed at six o'clock in the winter, and eight o'clock in the summer."

The monitors' boy, or secretary, enjoyed a sinecure; for his office was merely to help himself to a lion's share of what the monitors left: added to this, of course, he might sit up to attend to the monitors. This post was generally filled by a leading boy. Next to monitors' boy came monitors' boy's boy; who was supposed to polish the shoes, and the bones as well, but in reality he only looked after the latter; after him followed in a descending scale, the veritable fag, or monitors' boy's boy's boy, who, for a cold potato, or some execrable wash in the shape of tea, undertook to keep the crockery clean, scour out the cupboard, and was, in fact, a general scrub. His perquisites, if they warrant the name, were indeed hardly earned; but then, of course, he had a chance of one day being monitors' boy number one, or perhaps even monitor.

From Leigh Hunt's account it would appear that even in his day, when the discipline, as we have seen, was in every respect more harsh than now, the rule of the monitors was not particularly severe. He says:—

"I had not been long in the school when the spirit within me broke out in a manner that procured me great esteem. There was a monitor or 'big boy' in office, who had a trick of entertaining himself by pelting lesser boys' heads with a hard ball. He used to throw it at this boy and that; make the throwee bring it back to him, and then send a rap with it on his cerebellum, as he was going off.

"I had borne this spectacle one day for some time, when the family precepts rising within me, I said to myself, 'I must go up to the monitor and speak to him about this.' I issued forth accordingly, and to the astonishment of all present, who had never witnessed such an act of insubordination, I said, 'You have no right to do this.' The monitor, more astounded than any one, exclaimed, 'What?' I repeated my remonstrance. He treated me with the greatest contempt, as if disdaining even to strike me, and finished by ordering me to stand out. 'Standing out' meant going to a particular spot in the hall where we dined. I did so; but just as the steward (the master in that place) was entering it, the monitor called to me to come away; and I neither heard any more of standing out, nor saw any more of the ball. I do not recollect that he even 'spited' me afterwards, which must have been thought very remarkable. I seemed fairly to have taken away the breath of his calculations. The probability is that he was a good lad who had got a bad habit. Boys often become tyrants from a notion of its being grand and manly.

"Another monitor, a year or two afterwards, took it into his head to force me to be his fag. Fag was not the term at our school, though it was in our vocabulary. Fag with us meant eatables. The learned derived the word from the Greek phago, to eat. I had so little objection to serve out of love, that there is no office I could not have performed for good will; but it had been given out that I had determined not to be a menial on any other terms, and the monitor in question undertook to bring me to reason. He was a mild good-looking boy about fourteen, remarkable for the neatness, and even elegance, of his appearance.

"Receiving the refusal, for which he had been prepared, he showed me a knot in a long handkerchief, and told me I should receive a lesson from that handkerchief every day, with the addition of a fresh knot every time unless I chose to alter my mind. I did not choose. I received the daily, or rather nightly, lesson, for it was then most convenient to strip me, and I came out of the ordeal in triumph. I never was fag to anybody; never made anybody's bed or cleaned his shoes, or was the boy to get his tea, much less expected to stand as a screen for him before the fire, which I have seen done; though, upon the whole, the boys were very mild governors."

It would be a strange anomaly if the monitorial rule had grown more harsh since Leigh Hunt's day; and it is indeed certain that in the worst of times nothing like the tyranny exercised as a matter of course by the prefects of Winchester School ever prevailed in Christ's Hospital.

CHAPTER XI.

BEADLES.

THE Christ's Hospital beadle plays a very important part in school government. He takes the fledgeling in hand on his entrance to the school. He escorts the youngster to his preliminary or probationary home, keeps "watch and ward" at the gates to see he makes no exit without permission—has his "h'eye" upon him in the non-school hours—is the supervisor of his games and the guardian of his morals. In our time he was the money changer, the great high priest of toffee and the tuck-shop, the presiding genius at our ablutions and Peerless Pool excursions; the great bircher or executioner; the custodian of the bell which called us to our duties; the one link between the little world inside and the great world without, and the most gorgeously attired representative of the school on all public occasions.

In the original "orders of the Hospitals" the duties of the porter or head beadle are thus described:—

"You shall be attendant, diligente, and carefully in looking to the gates, chiefly in the winter evenings, and see them shut in at a due hour, and after they be shut in, to be circumspect whom you let in or out.

"Whereof assure yourselves without any favour or otherwise according to the governours' discretion."

It is of course needless to add that the duties of the beadle of the present day are totally different from those above described, and his attention is exclusively directed to duties within the gates.

The above is, however, interesting as showing the character of the school in its early days, before the foundation threw off its pauper surroundings.

As an evidence of the respect which the beadle commands both within and without the gates, we may mention that when on a recent occasion one of their number, Tice by name, retired from that position, which he had held for about thirty-three years, the old scholars presented him with a purse of seventy guineas as a tribute of their respect.

"There never was such a beadle," wrote a warm admirer, "and never will be again."

If Dickens had ever seen him, nay, if Mr. Trollope or Mr. Wilkie Collins could see him now, we should get put upon record the perfect picture of a beadle, not only as he exists in the glory of gold lace, which is a small matter, but with the attribute of a humour, such as Dickens was driven to imagine for Mr. Samuel Weller, and Thackeray for Jeames de la Plush. People who have seen a beadle of the right sort, for the real beadle is a *rara avis*, only seen once in a hundred years, have no conception from the feeble outlines supplied in the pages of Dickens what a beadle is.

Bumble was only a beadle of the cruel type; the beadle of Ipswich was only an ass of the pompous type.

But the beadle of Christ's Hospital is a pillar of the state, an essential part of the constitution.

How the beadle is first appointed we do not know,

we have never dared to inquire, for these are mysteries not to be revealed to the profane.

Another character was Nottley. This worthy rendered his name immortal from a graphic description of a fight which took place during our stay at Christ's Hospital.

"If you please, sir," said he to the steward, in reporting the case, "I found these two here a combattants a combattatting, and if I had not a conterfered the *hin*siquences would have been hawful."

On one occasion Nottley discovered a small boy sitting on the cold stones, when he remarked, "If you don't get up, I'll knock you down." A boy once asked him what a sarcophagus was?

"A sarcophagus? Why a sarcophagus, — well! well! well! well!—is a sarcophagus." But this did not satisfy the inquiring mind, and so the beadle was pressed to explain more in detail what a sarcophagus really did mean.

"Well," said Nottley, "since you must know what a sarcophagus is, I'll tell you, my little boy—it's a place where the dead men live."

Nurses.

Nurses, or matrons as they are now termed, have each a dormitory to superintend, and about fifty boys to look after. Our nurse was one of the old school, and though a little pronounced in her likes and dislikes, she was not on the whole so disagreeable and prone to reporting as some of the other nurses.

It oozed out that the 1st of May was Mrs. Hunt's natal day, and as sure as ever that memorable day came round, the youngsters, with a cruelly spiteful memory, would begin as early as five o'clock to "wish her joy,"—as that was the term we always used in birthday congratulations. Not content, how-over, with saluting the waking senses of the nurse with the words usually employed amongst themselves, the boys invented a doggerel, which ran thus:—

> "First of May, Chummy's day,
> Our old nurse's Birthday.
> Wish you joy, mum!"

Whether it was owing to the disrespect shown to the day—which was then kept with no ordinary degree of pomp—or whether Mrs. Hunt objected to be called old, we know not, but she used to threaten us with all sorts of "pains and penalties," if we persisted in our chorus of good wishes. And now a word as to the general duties of nurses. They are expected to give their "entire and ready attention" to the boys, to treat them with "kindness and forbearance, avoiding all railing, scolding, and immorality, and to enforce good manners, and respectful behaviour in the children committed to their care." They are required to "see that prayers are duly read before the boys go to bed, and that they go to bed at night and rise in the morning at the appointed time; to attend in the hall at meal times, for the purpose of carving and otherwise distributing the food; to report the absence of any boy or boys; never to absent themselves from the hall without the leave of the steward, nor from the Hospital without the leave of the treasurer." At a quarter before ten o'clock a bell summons the monitors and other privileged boys to bed, and shortly afterwards each nurse goes round her ward to see that the children are all in their beds and properly covered. The nurses were required at one time to "clean and keep sweet the great hall," but now they are relieved of that duty.

The matron, who is the immediate authority over the nurses, made periodical visits to the wards, to inspect the boys' beds, clothing, &c. The original charge in the order of 1557 runs thus:—" You shall twise or thrise in every weke arise in the night, and go as well into the sick warde, as also into every other warde, and there se that the children be covered in the beddes, whereby they take no cold."

On one occasion it was suggested by one of the youngsters that we should send the nurse a present, and a committee was forthwith formed, with extraordinary powers to decide upon the kind and manner of the presentation. After much discussion it was decided unanimously that we should, out of consideration for past services and present conduct, make up a hamper—a regular *bonâ fide* Christmas hamper. Opinions were divided as to the contents of the hamper, one boy voting in favour of filling it with dirty linen, whilst another suggested that a young donkey might be purchased for about 2s. 6d. All, however, agreed that the contents should be of a character to surprise the weak nerves of poor Mrs. Hunt. A young Scotch boy, who objected to any money being expended, suggested that a well-known cat belonging to one of the beadles might be pressed into the service. At length, after much discussion, a boy of the name of Richardson, who was one of the ringleaders in this affair, volunteered to go into the hamper himself, and the idea was rapidly caught up. A boy was sent off at once in quest of straw, whilst another was deputed to gather together all the rotten apples and pears he could collect. A few "dead men," in the shape of empty bottles, were speedily filled with water, and covered with dust and cobwebs, to do duty for "old port," and every minute arrangement was successfully carried out, to present Mrs. Hunt with a regular "bumper" of a hamper. Never was such a parcel made up with so much care. Young Richardson was placed most carefully at the bottom with a nice layer of straw over him; then followed the wine; then another layer of straw, and on the top came the apples, pears, and a few onions. The hamper was duly fastened, labelled, and directed, "Mrs. Hunt, No. 10 Ward, Christ's Hospital, London, with Mrs. Thompson's compliments, wishing Mrs. Hunt many happy returns of the season!" So heavy was the hamper, the old port no doubt contributing greatly to the weight, that it took four of us to carry it into the ward. On entering we set up a most fearful noise, all shouting at the top of our voice, "A parcel for Mrs. Hunt,"—who came rushing out of her cosy room with the greatest excitement and curiosity. "Take it into the kitchen," said the delighted recipient of the welcome present. "Mary," —the servant's name (for so were all Mrs. Hunt's servants christened, regardless of the wishes of godfathers or godmothers) "Mary, take in the parcel. I will be with you directly."

The girl, who had been let into the secret, neither replied nor put in any appearance, and for one very good reason—she was indulging behind the door in most immoderate laughter.

Without finishing her dinner, Mrs. Hunt, anxious to know the contents of such a weighty hamper, proceeded to the kitchen to examine her treasure. The boys crowded round the kitchen door to see how the joke would turn out. The string was then cut, and the label examined with much minuteness. On looking through the window we could see the countenance of the girl undergoing sundry strange contortions as the examination was proceeding. The first appearance of the apples, pears, and onions was evidently disappointing, but the poor old lady accounted for their appearance by stating her belief that the parcel had been delayed many days in transit. The "fine crusted port" gave great satisfaction, and the bottles were arranged on the dresser with conscious pride, and were counted over two or three times. Poor Richardson now began to feel the lightness of the upper region. He had heard all the conversation, and was prepared to play a bold game. Giving a most unearthly shout, to which the war-whoop of a savage would have been but as a whisper, he threw his legs high up into the air, and made a rush for the door. The boys received the hero with a tremendous shout, and from that day Richardson was idolised by the school. When Mrs. Hunt had recovered sufficiently to take stock of the situation, she repaired to the steward to complain of the treatment she had received. The kind-hearted steward, though strict enough when occasion required it, took a lenient view of the case, it being Christmas time, and, though he instituted inquiries, as in duty bound, to ascertain the leader in the affair, the boys, one and all, refused to divulge the secret, and Mrs. Hunt was never able to discover to whom she was indebted for her Christmas hamper.

CHAPTER XII.

SCHOOL SLANG AND LITERATURE.

HRIST'S HOSPITAL rejoices in a rare and extensive vocabulary of slang. Every public school has words peculiar to itself, but the scholars of Christ's Hospital can point to a magnificent collection of indigenous jargon which bristles at every point with etymological nuts, hard enough to puzzle the most profound scholar or the most successful spelling-bee competitor, and extensive enough to make up a small dictionary.

The editor of a future edition of the Slang

Dictionary would find pearls beyond price if he would only betake himself to the sombre cloisters of Christ's Hospital, and listen for a time to the echoes of the place.

Many words which were native to the school cloisters have in the course of time disappeared, and some have fallen into disuse even in the present generation. The comparative isolation which has always distinguished Christ's Hospital has favoured the accumulation, or rather the retention of characteristic words; and now that it is gradually emerging into the outside world, these are necessarily dropping away.

Ack, ick, &c., interj. Refusal of a request; *e.g.*, "Lend me your book." "Ack!" *i.e.*, "no."

Barnet, interj. "Humbug!" Now obsolete.

Bite, interj. A word of warning.

Boss, verb. To miss one's aim; to be short-sighted; then, to look at.

Boss, subst. A short-sighted person.

Brogues. Breeches.

Brush, verb. Flog. Euphemism.

Bunky, adj. Awkward, badly finished.

Cake, verb. To cane. Subst., a stroke with the cane.

Chaff, subst. A small article or plaything; *e.g.*, "a pocket chaff." Connected with chattel, chapman, &c.

Chaff, verb. To exchange small articles; probably connected with the substantive; *e.g.*, "Chaff me your knife." Also exclamation of joy; "Chaff!"

Chaff, adj. Pleasant, applied to reading; *e.g.*, "a chaffy book." Glad; "I *am* chaffy."

Crug, subst. A corruption probably of crust, in which sense it is used at Hertford. At London, however, it is used for crumb and crust alike. Hence—

Cruggy, adj. Hungry.

Cruganaler, subst. Orthography dubious. A biscuit given on St. Matthew's Day. We incline to the

School Slang and Literature. 97

following derivation. The biscuit had once something to do with those nights when bread and beer, with cheese, were substituted for bread and butter and milk. Thence the term "crug and aler." The only argument that daunts us is the remembrance that the liquid was never dignified with the name of ale, but was invariably called "the swipes." Another derivation is "hard as nails." It is then spelt "cruggy-nailer."

Cud, adj. Severe.

Cuddy, adj. Hard, difficult, of a lesson. Also Hertfordicè for "passy."

Fin, interj. The reverse of "Bags I," as "Fin the small court," *i.e.*, "I won't have." "Latin, "fendo."

Fudge, verb, trans. or intrans. To prompt a fellow in class, or prompt oneself in class artificially. Thence to tell; *e.g.*, "Fudge me what the time is."

Housey, adj. Belonging to the Hospital.

Jibbed, past participle passive. To get into a row. "He got jibbed for breaking windows." Hertford word. London equivalent, *twigged*.

Knave, subst. A dunce. Hertford equivalent, *knack*. Derivation, ignavus (?).

Knock up, verb. To gain a place in class. Trans. or intrans. "I knocked up," or "I knocked Jones up." The Hertford equivalent is *ox up*.

Lash, verb. To envy. Usually used in the imperative, as a taunt.

Lux, subst. A lux, a splendid thing; *e.g.*, "My knife is wooston a lux." Probably short form of luxuriant. Hertford word.

Nig, subst. A dodge.

Nigshious, adj. Ingenious. "A nigshious dodge."

Part, subst. A boy's meals.

Passy, adj. Severe, of a master. Short for passionate.

Paxy, adj. Bad, watery.

Poll, verb. To maltreat; to make impure. Short for pollute.

Pun out, verb, trans. or intrans. Inform against; "I'll pun out." "I'll pun you out." Exclusively a London word; the Hertford form is—

Pun, intrans., or *pun of*, trans. Etym. dub.

Scaff, subst. A selfish fellow. Connected with scaly and scabby, which are its adjectives.

Scaffy, small, deficient.

Scrub, verb. To write fast. "Scrub it down!"

Scrub, subst. Handwriting. Lat. scribere, write.

Scuttle, verb. To cry out under oppression with a view to attracting the notice of one in authority. Hence—

Scuttlecat, subst. One who scuttles. Both this and the preceding are Hertford words.

Snitch, subst. A term of contempt.

Spadge, subst. and verb. To walk affectedly, or an affected walk. Originally merely to walk. Latin, spatiari. Cf. German *spatzieren*.

Titch, verb and subst. A flogging. Hertford word.

Touchy. Rather. "Touchy a lux." Etym. bud.

Vex, adv. So much the worse for; *e.g.*, "vex for you." The opposite to this is "chaff," as "Chaff for you."

Wooston, adv. (Such is the spelling we have seen in a book: it is open to correction); pronounced *wissent*. Very. "Wooston a jolly fellow." "A wooston jolly fellow." "I am wooston chaffy." One ingenious person has suggested "wasn't it?" as the derivation of this remarkable word, used in the first sense, and then applied to the others. It may be or it may not. We should say it may not. Another proposes "worse than," originally used with bad words. But according to the recent researches of the Rev. J. Guillemard, once a Grecian here, it is a corruption of the old and not refined Shakesperian epithet *whoreson*.

There are also some words used amongst us in a wrong meaning, as *degraded*. "He is degraded to do so and so," *i.e.*, He feels it a degradation to do so.

Many of these words are more general at Hertford than here in London, where they are mostly confined to the lower classes. The vulgar are always the most conservative, and many classical English words which might be considered coarse now a days are used at the bottom of the school without offence. The words, however, in the above list do not appear ever to have been common English words.

The School has now its monthly magazine, appropriately entitled "The Blue," written by "Blues for Blues." It is doubtless written in blue ink; it has, or rather had, a blue cover, and is embellished with illustrations of youthful Blues indulging in various Blue sports, and though the youths have a Blue dress, their countenances wear anything but a blue expression. The magazine is most admirably got up and carefully edited, and is eminently entitled to the support, not only of the cloistered capless youths, but of the large army of old Blues outside the walls.

During my stay at Christ's Hospital we had no magazine, but we were not without school literature, for well do we remember two sea-stories, written by one of the boys, named respectively, "Ben Barnacle," and "Will Watch."

These two stories were brought out in weekly parts, and were published with great regularity. The tales were issued only to subscribers, who paid one quarter in advance, and the popular writer (whose productions were in our opinion infinitely superior to anything that Captain Marryatt or Fennimore Cooper ever penned) pocketed a large amount of ready cash.

CHAPTER XIII.

CHAFFING.

"CHAFFING," or bargaining, was carried on with much spirit in the school, and high prices ruled the market; brass buttons and silver watches; "parts" of bread and Easter "bobs;" mivores and mince-pies, it mattered not, all found a market.

"One holiday, as I returned homewards, writes a 'Blue' of our day, with a sixpence in my pocket, I was seized with a spirit of covetousness, and purchased, with intent to sell, a little round of toffee. That evening in bed I divided it into twelve pennyworths, wrapped these same neatly in paper, placed them beneath my pillow, and made my calculations. By next evening I should have a shilling, which would be two shillings the evening after, and then four, and then eight, and so on. It reminded me of the old sum about the nails of the horse-shoe. In a year I should have more money than I should know what to do withal. I should be richer than both my uncles put together. But stop; what, after all, was the use of money? Was not enjoyment the end of man? If I ate just six of my pennyworths, I could sell the other six and buy another cake; re-divide it; eat six pieces, and sell the other six; buy a third cake, a fourth cake, and so on for ever and ever. I had discovered a simple but sure method for living eternally at no cost on toffee. So I ate the first six pennyworths. And then I thought with what anxieties and troubles the pursuit of commerce was accompanied! Had I not already eaten my six pennyworths? Consequently I could not be any ways a loser. If I had ate the other six, should I not, without an effort, in one evening, have made a clear profit on myself of sixpence? The specious reasoning was conclusive to a willing judgment, and so I ate the remaining six pennyworths."

On cold nights there was always a brisk demand for tea and cocoa after the boys had gone to bed. The more fortunate fellows, who were allowed by virtue of their position in the school to sit up studying till the monitors' bell rang at a quarter to ten, always profited largely from this demand. Well do I remember on one occasion how my olfactory nerves were tantalised with the sweet fragrance of cocoa, and as cup after cup of the delicious decoction was being put away down the throats of the "Great Eras," and mathemat. fellows, we began to speculate how soon the "chaffing" time would commence. As the packet of cocoa became "small by degrees and beautifully less," it almost seemed as if my political economist had forgotten for a time the principles of his youth, and intended for once to make the whole of the profit on himself. We were soon undeceived thereon. Walking stealthily round the ward, he was seen to spill a spoonful of the precious liquid on the pillow-cases of all who had given themselves up to sleep. The names of the unlucky sleepers were all booked, and when morning came they were one and all reminded of the cup of cocoa supplied over-night. Protests were in vain, for did not the pillow-cases bear undisputed proof of the wretches' guilt?

In my time raisins were "chaffed" at thirty a-penny, and that tariff allowed the wholesale merchant who could command fivepence to clear about 300 per cent. Such prices were very properly regarded by B—— as tending to utter ruin—prejudicial alike to the best interests of the boys and to the advancement of commerce. Our young political economist was not long in putting the commerce of the school into a healthier and more lucrative channel. By a stroke of genius he did that which no boy had ever before attempted—he realised just 600 per cent. on a pound of raisins. And yet he bought the same quality raisins and kept to the established tariff. How, then, did he manage to realise just double the profit of other sellers? Anxious to advance the progress towards wealth of all our readers, we will communicate the mysterious secret—he cut them in half and sold them at night!

CHAPTER XIV.

HOLIDAYS AND FRIENDLESS BOYS.

HO that has been a "Blue" does not remember the joyous feelings with which we ushered in the month of August? What chalking of walls in June and July, and marking of almanacks! The general reader should be informed that a few years back Blue-Coat boys were only permitted to enjoy one month's leave of absence, and August was the month selected. It is not so now, as a long holiday is also given at Christmas. In each ward there were sixty beds, and two months before August, *turning over* commenced. This is nothing more nor less than turning over the bed and occupant of number sixty. The bedsteads are all numbered in each dormitory. My *turn* to-night, and yours to-morrow, were expressions frequently used as August approached, and were well understood. I believe the intensity of the *turn* increased as the holidays approached; nor was that an unnatural result. Occupants of the earlier numbers generally kept awake,

and when their turn came, gently guided their overthrow, and so escaped coming in contact with the iron bedstead. Any boys undertook the office, and none were permitted to escape,— excepting sometimes monitors and big boys.

THE FRIENDLESS BOY.

They had no happy homes to visit during the holidays, it is true, no loved ones to welcome them, no rich uncle to "tip them"; but, on the other hand, they had no home partings—no wrenching of social ties—no severance from the family circle—no descents to make from the land of "milk and honey" to the stony desert of school life. The friendless boy was always happy when we left him behind in the big school, and always happier when we returned.

He was then master of the situation. His holiday seemed to commence as ours left off.

He was the first to greet us on our return, and was always most profuse in his inquiries as to the health of our mother, and the well-being of our grandmother.

"Shall I clean your honour's boots?" says one. "Would you like your breakfast in bed to-morrow morning?" says another. "Shall I carry your honour's parcel?" says a third; but a small coin was an infallible way of stopping this running fire of impertinent inquiry.

But times are changed.

The friendless boys are now no longer allowed to remain in the school during the holidays, but are despatched by the authorities to the sea-side, where with a mild discipline they enjoy themselves thoroughly.

A STRAY TIP.

A visitor to Christ's Hospital will always find a

number of boys gathered round the gates. These may be called the waiters upon providence, and are always on the look-out for a stray tip. When a boy's friends go to see him it is always a matter of difficulty to find him at once amongst the scattered throng, and the difficulty of search is, of course, increased by the similarity of dress. As soon as these boys discover the name of the lad in quest, they rush off shouting through the cloisters and wards the name of the fortunate fellow, and when success at length crowns their efforts it is really amusing to see with what eagerness they hurry their "man" to the visitor, in the full hope and expectation of a tip, and seldom indeed are they sent empty away. I remember a gentleman who knew little of the school once caught sight of a little fellow whose coat was turned, and on the yellow lining of which was printed the dreaded letter T. Now S—— was a young prig. He had been detected putting his hand into other boys' pockets during the night, and abstracting therefrom the Easter shillings which the boys had received at the Mansion House. He was caned and condemned to wear the turned coat with the brand always accorded to a thief. The visitor was naturally surprised to see a boy dressed differently to the others, and inquired the reason. S——, who was a little fellow with a very old head on his shoulders, calmly assured his interrogator that he was a teacher—hence the letter T. The gentleman was so pleased that so young a boy should have been elevated to such an important position that he gave the young sinner half-a-crown, and young S—— was always seen after hanging about the gates, looking out for "tips."

CHAPTER XV.

SUNDAY AT SCHOOL AND THE INFIRMARY.

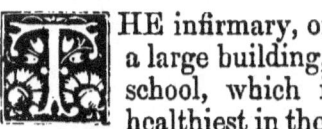HE infirmary, or sick ward, built in 1822, is a large building, far too large, in fact, for the school, which is, perhaps, statistically the healthiest in the country. There were seldom more than six or eight boys there together, but of course, it was a wise thing to anticipate the possible appearance of an epidemic. Our regular hours and habits, and healthy games, kept us from Mr. Stone's charge, but if anything could have reconciled us to the nauseous "purgo," it was the kind and courteous treatment of the surgeon, who was beloved by all in the school. Another gentleman whose name is a household word to sick "Blues" past and present, is Mr. Lancaster, one of the Governors. For more than thirty years Mr. Lancaster has made daily pilgrimage to the sick ward, where he is known to spend several hours, talking and reading, and generally amusing the poor sick children. He has, at his own expense, adorned the walls of the infirmary wards with choice and appropriate engravings, and his never-ceasing gifts of books must have cost him a small fortune. In addition to his Christian sympathy and help, Mr. Lancaster was a most practical benefactor, for he used to take us to baths for the purpose of teaching us to swim.

It was a real treat to get hold of Mr. Lancaster on Sunday, for our Sundays were dull, stale, and unprofitable, and it was fitly concluded by our singing the Burial Anthem. There was only one redeeming feature in connection with it—we rose an hour later.

A little before eleven we mustered under the

cloisters to await the steward's inspection, and the poor unlucky wight who had lost his Bible or wretched little cap was called out of the ranks by the steward or monitor to be punished on the morrow according to the heinousness of the offence. In the afternoon the monitors or markers heard us repeat the catechism or school hymns, and in the evening the Head Master gave us a sermon in the great hall. It was no joke to have a cough in those days, for Dr. Rice would, directly a boy commenced coughing, stop reading and sit down forthwith, remarking aloud, "I will sit down now until the boy who has just coughed has left the hall!" and the eyes of all would be turned upon the young culprit who had dared to disturb the doctor's serenity of mind.

After the evening discourse we repaired to our respective wards, when the monitors read a chapter of the Bible and the usual prayers, and then, as I have already remarked, we went to bed with the "Burial Anthem" ringing in our ears, and to this day I never hear the well-known words of the psalmist, "before I go hence and am no more seen," without thinking of the Christ's Hospital Sunday. It would be difficult, perhaps, to make the Sunday much brighter, but still I should like to see an attempt made. I am confident of this, that the attendance at morning service might be made less of a torture. The misery of kneeling out the "Litany" on hard boards was intolerable, and after our knee-buttons had been entering the flesh for what seemed to be hours, we were certainly in mood penitential and heartily joined in the exhortation, "Have mercy upon us, miserable sinners!"

D'Arcy Thompson, in giving his recollections of Christ's Hospital Sundays, says: "Whilst I am in church, I would fain record the impressions made upon me by a few memorable discourses. Upon the death of the incumbent, the curate preached a funeral sermon. His text was, 'We,' meaning the incumbent and himself, 'went up into the house of God together.' This statement amazed me exceedingly, for the incumbent had been a non-resident, and had never set eyes on the oldest boy amongst us. I inferred, however, that incumbent and curate had been in the habit of going through the services on week-days snugly and comfortably by themselves. At the close of his discourse, the preacher was so overcome with his own eloquence and the recollection of these religious *têtes-à-tête* that he was unable to lift his head off the cushion, and two churchwardens had to lead him by the arms down the pulpit stairs. It was touching beyond words to tell; but the occasion was nothing for pathos to that on which our friend, having failed in his candidature for the incumbency, preached as it were his own funeral sermon, dug his pulpit grave before our very eyes, got into it, and covered himself all over with the mould of words. Everybody wept, from great churchwardens and beadles down to common laymen and chits like myself. Not more universal was the world's sorrow at the death of Baldur, or the sobbing of the feathered creation at the murder of Cock Robin."

Attending Christ's Church on a recent occasion, I was pained to find that very little improvement whatever had taken place in the service; and to make matters worse, through extreme age, the much-respected vicar, the Rev. Michael Gibbs, was with difficulty able to make himself heard by the boys.

CHAPTER XVI.

EASTER CEREMONIES.—PUBLIC SUPPERS.

MONGST the characteristic features of Christ's Hospital are the Easter Ceremonies and Public Suppers, which are in some sense unique, while they always have been anticipated by the boys with peculiar pleasure and delight. In Passion Week a distribution of clothing took place, and the boys were granted a fortnight's holiday. The choice of the clothing used to be, and probably still is, an event exciting much interest, and the selection made often gave rise to abundance of criticism, or expressions of admiration, as the case might be.

As a matter of course Good Friday was observed with all due solemnity, and the day was specially marked by the quaint ceremony, described in the chapter on "Peculiar Bequests," and known amongst the boys as "chanting for a penny and singing for a plum." Easter was distinguished by the attendance of the Lord Mayor and Sheriffs at Christ's Church, and on the Monday and Tuesday the most interesting and imposing ceremonials of the year—in the estimation of the boys at any rate—took place. On the Monday we proceeded, accompanied by the masters, steward, and beadles, to the Royal Exchange, waiting there until we were summoned to the Mansion House. Arrived at the official residence of the great civic dignitary, we were joined by the Lord Mayor, Lady Mayoress, sheriffs, aldermen and other important functionaries, who marched with us in procession to Christ's Church, where a sermon was preached by one of the bishops, or by some divine of distinction, and we sang an appropriate anthem. To the breast of each boy was attached a label on which were inscribed the words "He is risen," by way of a reminder of the occasion of the festival. At the close of the service the Lord Mayor, the aldermen and their attendants returned to the Mansion House to dinner. On Tuesday our delightful excitement was at fever heat again; for then we once more visited the Mansion House to receive that which is always dear to the Blue heart—a "tip," and that a shining one. On reaching the state habitation—the palace, so to speak —of the civic king, we were passed on, one by one, to the Venetian parlour, where we found his lordship seated at a table surrounded by his friends. Close by the Lord Mayor's hand was a heap of new shillings, one of which was given as he passed the table to each boy, who was immediately handed by a servant in livery two buns, and by another a glass of wine—a ceremony observed to this day, and as much appreciated by the present as it formerly was by the past generations of "Blues." There are vague and wild traditions of boys who have succeeded by extraordinary ingenuity in securing a double allowance of buns and two glasses of wine, but these legends may be dismissed as improbable, and untrustworthy, and on the face of them belonging to the region of fable.

The Public Suppers, which again are characteristic of Christ's Hospital, took place every Sunday— they are now held every Thursday—evening during Lent, the admission being by a governor's ticket, the demand for which was always considerable. These suppers were looked forward to with much pleasure by the boys, not because there was any addition to their usual frugal fare, but because at such times the great hall presented a very animated appearance, being usually crowded with fashionably dressed visitors. In olden days the supper consisted of the usual allowance of bread, cheese, and very small beer; but in my time, as now, it was of bread and butter, milk and water, or, as we called it, "sky blue," being substituted for the beer.

At these public suppers cross and side seats were arranged at the top of the hall for visitors, according to their rank, the Lord Mayor, the sheriffs, and personages of distinction being sometimes in attendance. After the usual prayers the boys attacked the repast with all the eagerness of youthful appetite, the visitors the while promenading the spacious hall, and some of them chatting with their youthful friends amongst the hungry "Blues." Supper at an end the boys sang an anthem, always in admirable style, and then the important ceremony of "bowing round" began. The various wards formed themselves into ranks, headed by the nurses and monitors, and interspersed with a view of relieving what might otherwise have been monotonous in the proceedings, with the bearers of the bread basket, the knife basket, table cloths, water and beer cans, salt, bowls, and the smallest boys carrying candlesticks. At this ceremony, which lasted at least half-an-hour, either the Lord Mayor or one of the Governors presided, the boys, two and two, bowing as they passed the chair.

The office of president on these occasions is no sinecure, and though for the sake of the continuity of the traditions of the school, it is desirable that the "bowing round" should not be discontinued, the ceremony might well be shorn of its unfair proportions, in order to spare the Lord Mayor, or his representative for the time being, the painful necessity for keeping up a nodding acquaintance for an indefinite time, with all the "Blues of the period."

Charles Lamb, referring to the school festivities, ceremonies, and so forth, speaks of "our visits to the Tower, where, by ancient privilege, we had free access to all the curiosities; our solemn processions through the city at Easter, with the Lord Mayor's largess of buns, wine, and a shilling, with the festive questions and civic pleasantries of the dispensing aldermen, which were more to us than all the rest of the banquet; our stately suppings in public, where the well-lighted hall, and the confluence of well-dressed company, who came to see us, made the whole look more like a concert or assembly than a scene of a plain bread and cheese collation; and the annual orations upon St. Matthew's Day, in which the senior scholar, before he had done, seldom failed to reckon up those who had done honour to our school by being educated in it."

There was a ceremony, now happily long numbered among the things that have been, which at one time, by some strange freak of fortune, became connected with the School, and on that account deserves a passing notice here. About the middle of the last century, when lotteries were publicly and officially allowed, Blue-Coat boys were appointed to draw the tickets, and many attempts (some of which were successful) to tamper with the boys so employed could be instanced; and in 1775 the Lords of the Treasury issued some fresh rules and regulations, to prevent the boys committing frauds. By those rules the number of boys taking part in the lottery was increased from six to twelve, and managers were appointed whose duty it was specially to watch the movements of the two boys selected out of the twelve to preside at the wheel.

CHAPTER XVII.

BULLIES, FAGS, AND FAGGING.

 BULLY, *per se*, it will be readily admitted, by all except bullies, is not a pleasant personage, nor one whose acquaintance it is usually considered desirable to cultivate; but everywhere, in all countries, and in all ages, bullies have existed, and it is to be feared will continue to exist, as long as the world endures. As an American humourist truly observes, "there is a great deal of human nature in man," and the remark is equally true of the boy, "only more so," as the same humourist would probably have said if the question had been submitted for his consideration. Just as you see parliamentary bullies, legal bullies, official bullies, military bullies, domestic bullies, and—tell it not in Gath—even clerical bullies; so there are bullies in every public school, and, though they are far from numerous, as compared with the great bulk of the scholars, they are apt, unless carefully kept in check, to earn for the school a disagreeable reputation. In fact a bad deed "in a naughty world" is quite as apt to shine as a good one; and the misconduct of a few boys is bruited abroad as illustrative of the normal condition of things, while the ordinary routine, the wholesome discipline, and the quiet hard work of the school are apt to be forgotten. Of late years much of the rough horseplay which used to distinguish our great educational institutions, much of the brutality which, as a mere matter of course, was inflicted and endured, has disappeared; and we take leave to say that bullying and fagging were never, at Christ's Hospital, even in the worst of times, carried to any-

thing like the extent to which those practices prevailed in aristocratic institutions, such as Westminster, Eton, Harrow, and Winchester. There can be no doubt that practices do still prevail, founded on the old barbarous notion that a certain amount of ill-treatment is required to render a boy hardy, and to enable him to make his way in the world; but the idea—always a most mistaken one—is gradually dying out, and the sooner it disappears altogether the better it will be for the world in general, and for public schoolboys in particular.

Bullies—we speak here only of boy bullies—may be divided into two classes. There is the big, hulking, cowardly bully, in whom the vice is inherent by reason of his cowardice; the bully born, who can only be quelled by the strong hand, the firm eye, unceasing vigilance, and inflexible rigour; and there is the boy who becomes a bully rather from thoughtlessness and exuberant animal spirits than from any other cause. The case of the latter is hopeful; he is as likely as not to become a brave, modest, able, and considerate gentleman; the former is only too likely, to the end of the chapter, to oppress the weak and truckle to the strong. But bullying, from whatever cause it may originate, should be firmly repressed by the authorities of all schools, whether public or private; for a system of petty tyranny, continuously pursued, is apt to demoralise the oppressor as much as the oppressed; indeed, it works, and cannot fail to work, mischief "all round."

Fagging, as it is understood at Eton or Winchester, for instance, is almost unknown in the Blue-Coat School, except in the case of the Grecians' or monitors' boys, and even these young gentlemen have a comparatively easy time of it; the real drudgery, as we have shown in a preceding chapter, falling on the Grecian's, or (as the case may be) the monitor's boy's boy. Fagging, as we see it at the present day in Christ's Hospital, is after all only a relic of the old times, when the sons of the haughtiest nobles thought it no derogation from their dignity to serve in almost menial capacities the knights of fame to whose care their education was entrusted. Indeed fagging, in its modern and modified form, is chiefly objectionable on account of the bullying which, in the aristocratic public schools, is, or was, its almost inseparable accompaniment; and if the one cannot exist without the other, both, we venture to say, are doomed. The *régime* of the masters of the Blue-Coat School is now, as we have seen, of the very mildest kind, and of course it cannot be tolerated that amongst the scholars themselves any system of cruelty should exist. In the days of Dr. Boyer, when government of all descriptions, whether in the family, in public institutions, or in the state, was too often founded on a system of terrorism, there can be no question but that the younger and weaker boys were very often most harshly, if not cruelly treated. Speaking of the monitors of his own time, Charles Lamb says, "it must be confessed they had rather too much licence allowed them to oppress and misuse their inferiors; and the interference of the Grecian, who may be considered as the spiritual power, was not unfrequently called for, to mitigate by its mediation the heavy, unrelenting arm of this temporal power, or monitor. In fine, the Grecians were the solemn Muftis of the school."

And, a little later, he goes on to say, "As I ventured to call the Grecians the Muftis of the school, the King's boys" (the mathematical pupils), "as their character then was, may well pass for the Janissaries. They were the terror of all the other boys; bred up under that hardy sailor, as well as excellent mathematician, and co-navigator with Captain Cook, William Wales. All his systems were adapted to fit them for the rough element which they were destined to encounter. . . . . His punishments were a game at patience, in which the master was not always worst contented when he found himself at times overcome by his pupil. What success this discipline had, or how the effects of it operated upon the after lives of these King's boys, I cannot say; but I am sure that for the time they were absolute nuisances to the rest of the school. Hardy, brutal, and often wicked, they were the most graceless lump in the whole mass; older and bigger than the other boys, they were a constant terror to the younger part of the school."

Leigh Hunt, too, says of the Navigation School, "Upon the strength of cultivating their valour for the navy, and being called King's Boys, they had succeeded in establishing an extraordinary pretension to respect. This they sustained in a manner as laughable to call to mind as it was grave in its reception. It was an etiquette among them never to move out of a right line as they walked, whoever stood in their way. I believe there was a secret understanding with Grecians and Deputy Grecians, the former of whom were unquestionably lords paramount in point of fact, and stood and walked aloof when all the rest of the school were marshalled in bodies. I do not remember any clashing between these civil and naval powers; but I remember well my astonishment when I first beheld some of my little comrades overthrown by the progress of one of these very straightforward marine personages, who walked on with as tranquil and unconscious a face as if nothing had happened. It was not a fierce-looking push; there seemed to be no intention in it. The insolence lay in the boy not appearing to know that such inferior creatures existed."

Between the time of Leigh Hunt and my own time

a very considerable change for the better had taken place, but even then there was need of many improvements which have since been effected. An old schoolfellow of this later period gives one or two instances of bullying which are, probably, unique of their kind. "Poor honest Prior," he says, "gentle as a sheep, huge as a buffalo, slept next to a wolf of a bully, Smith. An evil conscience kept the former awake one night to an unusually late hour; when at length he roused up Smith, to tell him that the day had been his birthday, that a plum cake was in his settle, and that a slice was at his disposal. 'Had you told me of this before,' was the reply, 'I should have given you a bit.' As it was, the poor owner of the cake had to make it over *in toto* to the wolf, and had, moreover, to pass a considerable part of the night on the floor beneath his bed, for venturing to keep, over so many unnecessary hours, a secret of so important a nature."

Of another bully the same writer says:—" He gave a little boy an empty common stone ink-bottle—which, when full, would have cost one penny—to keep in charge, urging upon him the greatest possible caution. *Timeo Danaos et dona ferentes* would have passed through the little fellow's brain had he known enough of Latin at the time. At all events, the meaning of the words did pass through his mind, and for days the clumsy bottle was carried about in his pocket, and placed at night beneath his pillow. By-and-by he grew secure, and tired, and careless, and deposited the charge in his settle. Scarcely an hour elapsed before restitution was demanded. The culprit ran to his settle, but the deposit was gone. Trembling, he disclosed the fact to Turquand, who burst into well-simulated weeping, seized the defaulter by the hair, and shrieked, 'You little thief, that bottle was given me by my grandfather on his death-bed; you shall give me five shillings for it, or you'll break my heart!' He would have broken the little fellow's head if the promise of payment had not been instantly given. The money was paid in full, by instalments out of the child's pocket-money.

"In course of time the system became intensified in cruelty. The bullies, or *brassers*, as they were termed, were as terrible and as daring as Cilician pirates. On a general holiday they would be stationed near the gate, when the little fellows came home at evening from their visits, laden with cake and fruit, and rich with small silver coins. The majority of them would reach their beds with pockets as empty as they had left withal that morning. Some cautious urchins would devour all their treasures on the road, and would pay dearly—not too dearly—for their caution, or temerity. The evil at length became so flagrant that the cry of the oppressed went up to the ears of the head master; a special commission of inquiry was instituted; disclosures of the most appalling kind were made; condign vengeance was taken in public upon dozens of the pirates; and the land had rest for years, and has rest, I trust, to this day."

I remember, in the course of my own experience, a rather amusing case in which a boy belonging to my ward received a sound drubbing for disappointing what were considered, doubtless, the just expectations of his schoolfellows. He was a somnambulist, and had a habit of getting up "in the dead waste and middle of the night," or what was to us the corresponding hour, and going through a variety of extraordinary antics in his sleep. These nocturnal performances were generally attributed to fits of indigestion, occasioned by the cheese that the somnambulist was allowed for supper. As the rest of the ward considered our young friend's performances to be of an amazingly droll description, we one night, with the benevolent intention of giving him a more than ordinarily severe attack of dyspepsia, and so securing an entertainment of unsurpassed brilliancy, clubbed our "parts" of cheese together, and made him a present of them. The cormorant devoured all, and retired to rest in due course. But, alas for the vanity of human expectations! Throughout that livelong night, he, and he alone, of all the ward, slept the peaceful sleep of innocent childhood, and indulged in no somnambulistic freak whatever. Indignant at being thus monstrously defrauded of a performance for which they had, as it were, paid in advance, the boys next day wreaked summary vengeance on the defaulter, causing him bitterly to regret either that he had eaten so much cheese on the preceding evening, or that it had not had the customary effect.

Another occasion occurs to me in which the boys took the law into their own hands, though in this case the offender deserved his punishment. For the sake of getting some favour—I forget its exact nature—out of a schoolfellow, a lad whose father was steward to a distinguished nobleman, represented to the schoolfellow in question that the duke had taken a great liking to him, and intended calling on the next holiday and taking him out in the ducal carriage. The unsuspecting victim listened and believed, and no bride on her wedding morn could have been more particular about her dress than was the deluded one when the great day arrived. Eleven o'clock in the morning saw him in his best bib and tucker, with a coat on which was no speck of dust, and bands of spotless purity, waiting for the duke, who might have been the veritable Duke Humphrey himself, seeing the slenderness of the entertainment he provided. "From morn till noon, from noon till dewy eve," the confiding youth waited for the illustrious peer, who, it is needless to say, never arrived. Great was his wrath when he found that he had been too fondly credulous, and had lent a willing ear to one who was at best a gay deceiver. To a sympathising jury of his wardmates the victim told the story of his wrongs, and the punishment inflicted on the offender induced a tenderness of feeling that led him to be very careful as to the fashion in which he hoaxed his schoolfellows in future.

Lamb himself is careful to show us how highly he estimates the character and conduct of the youths educated on the foundation. "The Christ's Hospital or Blue-Coat boy," he says, "has a distinctive character of his own, as far removed from the abject qualities of a common charity-boy, as it is from the disgusting forwardness of a lad brought up at some other of the public schools. There is *pride* in it, accumulated from the circumstances which I have described as differencing him from the former; and there is a *restraining modesty*, from a sense of obligation and dependence, which must ever keep his deportment from assimilating to that of the latter. His very garb, as it is antique and venerable, feeds his self-respect; as it is a badge of dependence, it restrains the natural petulance of that age from breaking out into overt acts of insolence. This produces silence and a reserve before strangers, yet not that cowardly shyness which boys mewed up at home will feel: he will speak up when spoken to, but the stranger must begin the conversation with him. Within his bounds he is all fire and play; but in the streets he steals along with all the self-concentration of a young monk. He is never known to mix with other boys; they are a sort of laity to him. All this proceeds, I have no doubt, from the continual consciousness which he carries about him of the difference of his dress from that of the rest of the world; with a modest jealousy over himself, lest, by over-hastily mixing with common and secular playfellows, he should commit the dignity of his cloth. Nor let any one laugh at this; for, considering the propensity of the multitude, and especially of the small multitude, to ridicule any thing unusual in dress—above all, where such peculiarity may be construed by malice into a mark of disparagement—this reserve will appear to be nothing more than a wise instinct in the Blue-Coat boy. That it is neither pride nor rusticity, at least that it has none of the offensive qualities of either, a stranger may soon satisfy himself by putting a question to any of these boys: he may be sure of an answer couched in terms of plain civility, neither loquacious nor embarrassed."

Strangers very often do put questions to the boys, and conclude a conversation with the proverbial tip.

But not so was it with one old gentleman who once stopped a Blue in Cheapside, and inquired in the most patronising manner imaginable, putting his hand on the boy's head—

"Well, my little boy, and what *might* your name be?"

"Well," said the boy, nothing daunted, "*it might* be Beelzebub, but it isn't."

The proverbial tip was not forthcoming in this case; but the answer, pert as it undoubtedly was, proves at any rate that the spirit of the hopeful youth had not been broken by the manners and customs of Christ's Hospital.

CHAPTER XVIII.

THE TRADES.—" HOUSEY MONEY."—THE TUCK SHOP.

THE reader who has never sported the blue and yellow is begged not to infer rashly because trades are spoken of in relation to Christ's Hospital, that the institution is in any respect an " Industrial School," as that term is at present understood; nor does the word "trades" bear the precise significance that an outsider would naturally attach to it. It is a "trade," for instance, to carry candlesticks, to clean knives, to serve out salt, and in my time some of the trades not only conferred a certain distinction on those belonging to them, but really afforded the fortunate youths some more or less substantial benefits. A new boy on his introduction to a ward is very often puzzled by being put to a "trade," which in an ordinary household would fall to the lot of a parlour maid, a footman, or a servant-of-all-work, as the case may be. If the boy is very young or very diminutive, he is probably first employed as a bearer of candlesticks, or, if he should happen to be a favourite of the nurse, the very easy task of carrying the salt-bowl to the hall and serving out the salt may devolve upon him. Some of the trades are much sought after, while others, which involve a great deal of work, without bringing any corresponding advantage, are, as a matter of course, highly unpopular. A favourite post is that of trencher boy, or meat bearer, and with good reason, for the lucky holder of the office can always command an extra supply, and exercise a little private patronage (in the shape of gravy) for the benefit of his particular friends. The bread boy, too, unless he is much more dull than boys in general so far as eatables are concerned, can manage to secure some trifling perquisites of office which render him an object of envy to less favoured creatures with ordinary allowances and extraordinary appetites. The potato boy, likewise, is generally supposed to have what our American cousins would call a " good time," seeing that, on a cold day especially, a few extra hot potatoes are by no means to be despised. The duty of cleaning the knives and forks for sixty boys is not one that, at first sight, would seem likely to be sought for, but it is nevertheless in great demand, and the post of knife cleaner is generally held by an upper boy, who is responsible for the safe keeping of these weapons of gastronomic warfare. The popularity of this office is due to the nature of the reward conferred on the holder, which is nothing less than a ticket of leave to see his friends every Saturday afternoon. The post is necessarily no sinecure, but the haughty aristocrat on whom it is conferred engages one or more fags to do the real work. The unpopular trades, such, for instance, as cloth-boy, beer-boy, water-carrier, plate-boy, and bowl-boy, fall to the lot of new comers, and apprenticeship to one or other of the trades forms an inevitable incident in the Blue-Coat boy's career.

The boys for the various trades are appointed by the monitors, who are influenced in their choice by good behaviour, proficiency in the grammar school, and so forth. The boys of each trade are held responsible for the articles confided to their care.

In my time the buttery, which was beneath the cloisters of the great hall, was under the immediate guardianship of three boys appointed by the steward. These buttery boys were always monitors; the senior managed the bread department; the second was clerk of the dairy, and kept the accounts of the butter and cheese; and the third, as head cellarman, looked after the beer. These three boys were virtually clerks to the steward, and to be selected for a place in the buttery was considered a very high honour, while the dignity brought with it a reward in the shape of permission for the office-holders to see their friends every Saturday after dinner. As a matter of course the steward provided everything that was necessary for the daily consumption of the inmates of the School, but the after weighing was left entirely to the buttery boys, who were always supposed to be good penmen and quick at figures. The young gentlemen of the buttery, besides the advantage of the Saturday afternoon leave, had the means of procuring many little enjoyments which were wholly beyond the reach of their less fortunate schoolfellows, unless indeed they happen to be the particular chums of these heads of departments. They got, for instance, an extra quantity of rations, a choice of the best tap of table beer, and various other little perquisites of a description that never yet came amiss to hearty, hungry schoolboys. They were frequently able to give a snug little dinner party, taking care, of course, to be waited upon—as befitted their importance—by three or four of the juniors, who were duly rewarded for their services with the remains of the feast.

The tuck shop, at which almost anything could be purchased that the average schoolboy was likely to desire, was a great institution in my day; and it is, I hear, equally popular now under the management of the genial Fletcher, otherwise Johnny. Cakes, puffs, tarts, fruit, needles, thread, writing paper, pocket-knives, marbles, tops, and toys in general were, and are, to be procured here; and it need hardly be said that in so large an assemblage of boys the tuck shop never languished for lack of custom. In my time, singular as it may appear, these delicacies were not procurable by the Blue-Coat boy in return for the current coin of the realm. By an ancient custom, which is now abolished, we had a currency peculiar to ourselves, the money issued from Her Majesty's mint not being a legal tender within the walls of Christ's Hospital. No; in this respect the foundation had an institution of its own—an institution by which it was distinguished from all other educational establishments, large or small, public or private, endowed or unendowed, within the realm of Britain. This institution, this current coin of our own little territory, was known by the curious name of "Housey money," and it was illegal for boys to make purchases outside the gates, or to retain in their possession any pieces of money bearing "the golden" (or silvern, as the case might be) "round and top of sovereignty." When, therefore, a boy out on leave was tipped, he had, on returning to the Hospital, to seek out the money-changer (one of the beadles) and exchange the coin of the realm for copper coins of an octagonal form, having impressed upon them the amount of their purchasing power, which was the value they were supposed to represent. Then, and not till then, could the tuck shop be visited, and a supply of its tempting delicacies procured. But this peculiar currency is done away with now. "Housey money" has gone the way of all coin; and probably no specimen of it is to be found in any numismatic collection extant, unless it be in that of some enthusiastic "old Blue" who keeps the battered piece of copper to remind him of "the light of other days."

CHAPTER XIX.

AMICABLE, BENEVOLENT, AND OTHER "BLUES."

NOW all the world knows something of the *esprit de corps* existing amongst all "Blues." The word "Crug" has a magical influence. To be a "Brother Crug" is to be a mason without mystery—a "brother" without expense. The word "Crug" can procure temporary help in youth and seasonable support in old age. It is a passport to friendship—a badge of distinction—a recaller of pleasant memories. It has given clergymen livings, supplied the barrister with briefs, the medical man with patients, and the business man with customers. It is known, honoured, loved, and respected wherever it is uttered, is this word "Crug."

Perhaps the two proudest monuments of "Brother Crug's" usefulness and beneficent character are the friendly societies known respectively as the "Amicable Society of Blues," and "The Benevolent Society of Blues." The former was established, I believe, about the year 1775, and the latter in 1824.

The Amicable is composed chiefly of the more successful and wealthy "Old Blues," and has been the means of relieving many a distressed and fallen "brother." The younger association, the "Benevolent Society of Blues," was started at 13, Maiden Lane, Covent Garden, in the year named, by twenty-two "Old Blues," who enrolled their names in a book which is still in the possession of the society.

After somewhat of a struggle, the capital fund was, on 3rd October, 1827, raised to the long-desired amount of £1,000 Consols, and at their November meeting in that year the Board received and inquired into seven applications for assistance. In October, 1829, the capital had increased to £2,000 Stock; in 1833, to £3,000 Stock; in 1841, to £5,050 Stock; in 1849 (April 25), to £6,900 Stock; and in 1869, it had increased to £20,000.

The total amount expended in forty-five years is as follows: In gifts, £7,795 17s. 1d.; in pensions, £8,554 9s. 9d.; advanced in loans, £1,417. During the same period the subscriptions and donations have amounted to £25,310 9s. 5d.; dividends, £9,300 8s. 1d.

It will thus be seen that a great work has been successfully carried on by the Society, and most heartily do we commend it to the support of all "Old Blues."

Annually, on the anniversary of King Edward's birthday, the old boys dine together; and these reunions are of the most enjoyable description. An old Blue of distinction generally occupies the chair.

THE END.

BRADBURY AGNEW, & CO., PRINTERS, WHITEFRIARS.

ADVERTISEMENTS.

PAINLESS DENTISTRY.

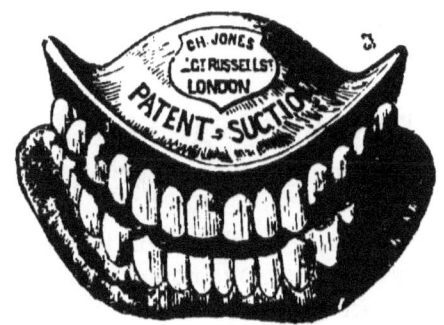

ARTIFICIAL TEETH.
MR. G. H. JONES,
Surgeon Dentist,
57, GREAT RUSSELL STREET, LONDON
Immediately opposite the British Museum,

HAS OBTAINED

HER MAJESTY'S ROYAL LETTERS PATENT

For his perfectly painless system of adapting Prize Medal (London and Paris)

ARTIFICIAL TEETH BY ATMOSPHERIC PRESSURE.

PAMPHLET GRATIS AND POST FREE.

NOTE.—Improved PRIZE MEDAL TEETH (London and Paris) are adapted in the most difficult and delicate cases, on a perfectly painless system of self-adhesion, extraction of loose teeth or stumps being unnecessary; and, by recent scientific discoveries and improvements in mechanical dentistry, detection is rendered utterly impossible, both by the close adjustment of artificial teeth to the gums and their life-like appearance. By this patented invention complete mastication, extreme lightness, combined with strength and durability, are ensured; useless bulk being obviated, articulation is rendered clear and distinct. In the administration of nitrous-oxide gas, Mr. G. H. Jones has introduced an entirely new process.

TESTIMONIAL.

"My dear Sir.—Allow me to express my sincere thanks for the skill and attention displayed in the construction of my Artificial Teeth, which renders my mastication and articulation excellent. I am glad to hear that you have obtained her Majesty's Royal Letters Patent, to protect what I consider the perfection of Painless Dentistry. In recognition of your valuable services, you are at liberty to use my name.

"G. H. JONES, Esq."
"S. G. HUTCHINGS, by appointment Surgeon-Dentist to the Queen.

ADVERTISEMENTS.

The Birkbeck Building Society's Annual Receipts exceed Four Millions.

HOW TO PURCHASE A HOUSE FOR TWO GUINEAS PER MONTH,

With Immediate Possession and no Rent to pay.—Apply at the Office of the BIRKBECK BUILDING SOCIETY, 29 & 30, Southampton Buildings, Chancery Lane.

HOW TO PURCHASE A PLOT OF LAND FOR FIVE SHILLINGS PER MONTH,

With Immediate Possession, either for Building or Gardening purposes.—Apply at the Office of the BIRKBECK FREEHOLD LAND SOCIETY, 29 & 30, Southampton Buildings, Chancery Lane.

HOW TO INVEST YOUR MONEY WITH SAFETY.

Apply at the Office of the BIRKBECK BANK, 29 & 30, Southampton Buildings, Chancery Lane. Deposits received at varying rates of interest for stated periods, or repayable on demand.

Current Accounts opened with parties properly introduced, and Interest allowed on the minimum monthly balances. English and Foreign Stocks and Shares purchased and sold, and Advances made thereon.

Office hours from 10 to 4; except on Saturdays, when the Bank closes at 2 o'clock. On Mondays the Bank is open until 9 o'clock in the Evening.

A Pamphlet, with full particulars, may be had on application.

FRANCIS RAVENSCROFT, Manager.

ADVERTISEMENTS.

STUART-BARKER & SON,

Surveyors and Auctioneers,

36, KING WILLIAM STREET,

LONDON BRIDGE, E.C.

"The METROPOLITAN PROPERTY REGISTER" is issued Monthly, and may be obtained free upon application.

TIC-DOULOUREUX, RHEUMATIC PAINS IN THE HEAD, FACE, OR TEETH, SCIATICA, NEURALGIA, ETC.

HOWELL'S
ANTI-NEURALGIC DROPS

Are a safe and effectual remedy. Warranted not to contain Colchicum, Opium, or any of its preparations. Prepared by

MAURICE HOWELL,
61, HIGH STREET, PECKHAM, S.E

In Bottles at 1s. 1½d. *and* 2s. 9d. *each.*

Sold Wholesale and Retail by Messrs. Newbery & Sons, 37, Newgate Street, E.C., and all Medicine Vendors. A bottle will be sent to any address, n receipt of 16 p°stage stamps, by the Proprietor.

ADVERTISEMENTS.

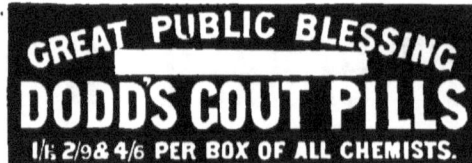

DODD'S
PULMONIC COUGH SYRUP,

A SAFE AND EFFECTUAL CURE FOR

Coughs, Colds, Shortness of Breath, Influenza, and all Complaints of the Chest and Lungs.

Prepared and Sold in Bottles, 1s. 1½d. and 2s. 9d. each, by

DODD & PYWELL, Surgeons & Apothecaries,
244, WESTMINSTER BRIDGE ROAD, LONDON.
Sold by all Chemists.

CHLORODYNE.
D^R. J. COLLIS BROWNE'S
THE ORIGINAL AND ONLY GENUINE.

CHLORODYNE is admitted by the Profession to be the most wonderful and valuable remedy ever discovered.
CHLORODYNE is the best remedy known for Coughs, Consumption, Bronchitis, Asthma.
CHLORODYNE acts like a charm in Diarrhœa, and is the only specific in Cholera and Dysentery.
CHLORODYNE effectually cuts short all attacks of Epilepsy, Hysteria, Palpitation, and Spasms.
CHLORODYNE is the only palliative in Neuralgia, Rheumatism, Gout, Cancer, Toothache, Meningitis, &c.

From LORD FRANCIS CONYNGHAM, *Mount Charles, Donegal,* 11*th December,* 1868.
"Lord Francis Conyngham, who this time last year bought some of Dr. J. Collis Browne's Chlorodyne from Mr. Davenport, and has found it a most wonderful medicine, will be glad to have half-a-dozen bottles sent at once to the above address."

"EARL RUSSELL communicated to the College of Physicians that he received a despatch from Her Majesty's Consul at Manilla, to the effect that Cholera had been raging fearfully, and that the ONLY remedy of any service was CHLORODYNE."—*See Lancet,* 1st December, 1864.

CAUTIONS.—BEWARE OF PIRACY AND IMITATIONS.

CAUTION.—Vice-Chancellor Sir W. PAGE WOOD, stated that Dr. J. Collis Browne was, undoubtedly, the Inventor of Chlorodyne; that the story of the Defendant Freeman was deliberately untrue, which he regretted to say had been sworn to."—*See Times,* 13th July, 1864.

Sold in Bottles at 1s. 1½d., 2s. 9d., and 4s. 6d. each. None is genuine without the words "Dr. J. COLLIS BROWNE'S CHLORODYNE," on the Government Stamp. Overwhelming Medical testimony accompanies each bottle.

Sole Manufacturer—
J. T. DAVENPORT, 36, GREAT RUSSELL ST., BLOOMSBURY, LONDON.

ADVERTISEMENTS.

ATHLETIC AND BRITISH SPORT REQUISITES. *Illustrated Prospectus post free.*
CHAS. SPENCER & CO., 2, Old St. (corner of Goswell Rd.), London.

D'ALMAINE'S PIANOS
AT HALF PRICE.

In consequence of the death of the late Proprietor, this splendid Stock of

NEARLY 500 PIANOFORTES
IS OFFERED AT
15 and 17 Guineas, worth 30 and 35 Guineas.

DOUBLE-CHECK ACTION TRICHORDS,
ALL AT HALF PRICE,
SPEEDY CLEARANCE REQUIRED AND EASY TERMS ARRANGED.
An opportunity that does not offer in every lifetime.
SEVEN YEARS' WARRANTY SECURED.

ADVERTISEMENTS.

ST. MARY'S COLLEGE,

A MIDDLE CLASS SCHOOL FOR BOYS.

HANOVER PARK, PECKHAM RYE, S.E.

(In union with the Church of England Middle Class Committee.)

VISITOR,
THE LORD BISHOP OF WINCHESTER.

WARDENS,
REV. M. BIGGS, M.A., ST. MARY MAGDALENE, PECKHAM.
REV. J. FLEMING, B.D., ST. MICHAEL'S, CHESTER SQUARE.
REV. G. K. FLINDT, M.A., ST. MATTHEW'S, DENMARK HILL.
REV. J. H. HAZELL, M.A., ST. ANDREW'S, PECKHAM.
REV. J. RICHARDSON, M.A., CAMDEN CHURCH, PECKHAM.

This School has been established to provide, at a moderate charge, a superior Commercial and Classical Education, on Church of England principles.

The course of Instruction comprises the English, French, Latin, and Greek Languages, History and Geography, Mathematics, Freehand, Model, and Geometrical Drawing, Linear Perspective, Vocal Music, Drilling, and Gymnastics.

Pupils intended for Commercial pursuits receive a special training in Arithmetic, Book-keeping, English and French Correspondence, and are taught to write a good Mercantile hand.

Classes are formed for the convenience of Candidates preparing for the Oxford or Cambridge Local Examinations.

The year is divided into three terms of 14 weeks each, beginning January 11, April 26, and September 13. There are vacations of three weeks at Christmas, one week at Eastertide, and six weeks in the Summer.

The Fees, which include the use of Class Books, Stationery, and Drawing Materials, are Eight and Six Guineas per annum, according to position in the School. These Fees are payable termly, *in advance.*

Pupils may enter at any time, on payment of the Fee for the unexpired portion of the Term.

EXTRA SUBJECTS.

Instruction in German or Italian can be had at the rate of One Guinea, and on the Pianoforte at the rate of Four Guineas, per annum.

Classes will be formed, when desired, for Levelling, Theodolite Surveying, and Practical Chemistry.

SCHOLARSHIPS.

The Committee of "St. Mary's College Scholarship Fund" offer annually (under specified restrictions) a certain number of Scholarships to pupils in attendance at the College. Particulars may be had of the Head Master, C. E. MOYSE, ESQ., B.A., or of the Honorary Secretary, Mr. WM. HARNETT BLANCH, author of "School Life in Christ's Hospital," "History of Dulwich College," &c., who can confidently recommend St. Mary's College as "one of the best conducted and most successful Middle Class Schools in the country. The accommodation for Boarders is excellent."

Arrangements are made by which Pupils from a distance can dine at the College, at an extra charge of £1 15s. per Term.

The Head Master receives a limited number of Boarders. Terms may be had on application to him.

St. Mary's College is within three minutes' walk of Peckham Rye railwa

ADVERTISEMENTS.

RECENTLY PUBLISHED.

THE HISTORY AND ANTIQUITIES OF CAMBERWELL. Price One Guinea.

THE HISTORY OF DULWICH COLLEGE.

With a Memoir of the Founder. Price 3s. 6d.; extra bound, suitable for a Prize or Present, 5s.

THE BLUE-COAT BOY; or School Life in Christ's Hospital. Beautifully bound, suitable for a Present. Price 5s.

Opinions of the Press on the "History of Camberwell."

"It is a marvellous book, and will make Mr. Blanch's name famous for generations."—*Educational Reporter.*

"Mr. Blanch has written a book which entitles him to rank with the historians."—*South London Press.*

"Concerning the past Mr. Blanch has written with laudable fidelity, concerning the present with commendable delicacy, and concerning the future with judicious reserve.—*Bell's Weekly Messenger.*

"Mr. Blanch has done good service, not merely to the parishioners of Camberwell, but to all who take an interest in metropolitan topography. Every Londoner must be interested in the book. It is a painstaking, interesting, and highly creditable production."—*City Press.*

"The book contains much that is valuable. Mr. Blanch gives us some startling figures concerning the growth of Camberwell."—*Saturday Review.*

"The historian's patient industry is worthy of all praise."—*Athenæum.*

"The work is admirably got up, and Camberwell should be proud of it."—*European Mail.*

"Mr. Blanch has executed his task with great diligence and discretion. We can only hope that the residents of Camberwell, Peckham, and Dulwich, may extend a patronage to the undertaking proportionate to the time and labour which must have been bestowed upon it."—*Standard.*

"A handsome volume, exhibiting exhaustive research."—*Graphic.*

"Written in most excellent English."—*Manchester Evening Mail.*

"Mr. Blanch has executed his work well, and added a volume to our local histories which will be a valuable addition to the library shelf."—*Plymouth Daily Mercury.*

"Mr. Blanch, the Assistant-Overseer of the parish of Camberwell, has made a valuable contribution to topographical history. It is an admirable work."—*News of the World.*

"Mr. Blanch's zeal is most praiseworthy, and the parish of Camberwell has received a measure of notice which has not fallen to the lot of many suburban districts. If anything has been omitted, it is beyond such testing as we could apply, for it has answered all our inquiries."—*Notes and Queries.*

"Mr. Blanch's history of old Camberwell families is not only complete, but perfectly marvellous. His book is an immense mine of wealth."—*Camberwell and Peckham Times.*

"Contains a vast amount of highly interesting information, suitable to the mental palate of the historian, antiquarian, and even the devourer of romance."—*Metropolitan.*

"The volume appears in every way most commendable, and exhibits proofs of energy, industry, and research."—*Illustrated London News.*

To be had of MR. WM. HARNETT BLANCH, 55, Denman Road, Peckham; and of E. W. ALLEN, Ave Maria Lane, E.C.

www.ingramcontent.com/pod-product-compliance
Lightning Source LLC
Chambersburg PA
CBHW030334170426
43202CB00010B/1120